TEACHING FOR SUCCESS

Effective Insights and Strategies

for Teaching

in Jewish Religious Schools

By

Dorothy C. Herman

Torah Aura Productions

Torah Aura Productions
4423 Fruitland Avenue
Los Angeles, California 90058
(800) BE-TORAH or (213) 585-7312

MANUFACTURED IN THE UNITED STATES OF AMERICA

Dedication

For my four sons—
Richard, Greg, Stuart, and Adam
and all of the
Temple Beth Am Religious School students
that I have had the pleasure to teach.

Editor's Note on Gender

Some students are males, some are females. The same is true of teachers, parents, principals, and even generic "people." For the sake of convenience (and because "s/he" is awfully awkward), even-numbered chapters of this work will employ feminine pronouns for all generic cases, odd-numbered chapters will utilize masculine pronouns. In order to be fair and completely nondiscriminatory, odd and even were determined by reversing the order taken in Mrs. Herman's first book, *Planning for Success*.

TABLE OF CONTENTS

1.

PLANNING FOR EFFECTIVE TEACHING

When I was a child in Religious School I always knew what to expect. Each week I would come into class and take my assigned seat. Each week the teacher would tell us to open our textbook and we would begin the lesson. The student in the first seat would read paragraph one. The student in the second seat would read paragraph two. The student in the third seat would read paragraph three. I was in the seventh seat, so, of course, the seventh paragraph always belonged to me. As the others before me were reading, I would quickly turn to paragraph seven and read it to myself, checking to see that I could pronounce all of the words so that I could read letter perfect when it was my turn. The teacher would ask us questions based on the readings when we completed each section. Religious School was so boring, but I knew that the material was worthwhile. I wished that it could be presented in a more dynamic fashion.

As I reflect on my Religious School experience I realize that I always knew what would happen in class and I knew what was expected of me. Today, religious education is different. Teachers are better prepared to use innovative methodology. They know that children learn in different ways and they try to accommodate each child whenever possible. This is a more difficult task than the one my Religious School teacher faced. When one ventures into the creative, one also has to be aware of impending discipline problems. Teachers need to prepare detailed directions for student involvement, and for student reaction to the curriculum. Students still need to know what is expected of them so that they can cooperate and reap the most benefit from the experience.

2.
ACHIEVING SUCCESS IN THE CLASSROOM

uccess in the classroom comes from the following:

Knowing who you are as a person and as a teacher.

Knowing what your expectations are and how you will realize them.

Being prepared with knowledge, methodology, discipline, and administrative skills.

Being flexible, but not flighty.

Having a feeling of accomplishment.

Enjoying children and the challenge of teaching them.

It is important that before you go into a classroom and face 15-25 children, you do your homework. Ask these questions. Find the answers.

1. What grade level will you be teaching? How old are the students? What are the characteristics of a child this age? What growth stages come before and after this age? Remember that not all children of the same age grow and mature at the same rate.

2. What curriculum will you be expected to teach? What are the objectives? Is there a set time frame in which you must complete the objectives? What materials are available? What help can you expect from the administrator or other teachers?

3. Is there a teacher's handbook, parent's handbook, and/or student's handbook? If there are, read and study these documents. They will list the school's goals and philosophy. They should list the curriculum throughout the school. These will help you to know what your students have been exposed to previously and what they will cover in the future. The rules of the school and discipline policies should be included.

4. What type of synagogue is it? Reform, Conservative, Orthodox, Reconstructionist? How will the institution's philosophy affect what and how you teach? Are your own beliefs consistent with those of the synagogue? If not, can you really teach there? Are there things that you cannot do if you accept a position with this school? (Shop on Shabbat, work as a bartender, teach at another school?)

5. What is the socioeconomic state of the families? Do both parents work? Is it a professional community? Do families take weekend vacations during the school year on a regular basis? Are many congregants recent immigrants?

6. Is there a high proportion of interfaith marriage in the congregation? Are there many Jews by choice? How will this affect the way in which you teach or what you can teach?

7. Is there a high rate of single parent families? Is there shared custody? Will children be visiting the noncustodial parent every other weekend? How does the synagogue accommodate this situation?

8. Do the members of the congregation observe traditions in their home? Do most of the Jewish experiences in the child's life happen in the synagogue or does the school reinforce the practices of the home?

9. Is there a major sport in the community that occurs during school time? Professional football or baseball? Children's football, baseball or soccer? How will these affect attendance? What is the school's policy?

10. Is there an attendance policy for bar/bat mitzvah? For Confirmation? How do people know about it and how is it enforced? How will this affect you?

11. What are the discipline policies of the school? What are you permitted to do? Do the parents and students know the policy? Can a child be suspended, expelled, denied bar/bat mitzvah or Confirmation? How are children disciplined? Can a child be sent to the office if his behavior is not acceptable? Will the principal support you?

12. What arrangements are made for the learning-disabled child or special-needs child? How can you find out about specific problems that a child may have? Are there cumulative records?

13. Who are the support people on staff? Will you have a student assistant? What are the policies for working with these assistants? Are there a library and librarian available? How can you utilize both? What audiovisual equipment is available? Will someone run it for you or teach you how to use it? Is there a copy machine that you can use? Will the school secretary type materials and tests for you? Is there an art teacher? Are there art supplies? How do you get what you need? Are there specialists for music, drama, dance? How can you utilize them? Is a rabbi available? In what special programs will your class participate? What is your responsibility?

14. Are there extra meetings that you will be expected to attend? How long before and after school should you be on campus?

15. Is it possible for your class to have a cooking experience? Can you bring in food for holidays or parties? Can you go on field trips? Is there a budget line for guest speakers?

16. Does the school have a buddy system for new teachers? Is there another teacher who is teaching on the same level or who is teaching the same material?

17. If you are absent, who secures the substitute teacher? What is the substitute supposed to do?

18. Are you responsible for giving exams? Are report cards issued? How many times a year are they distributed? Secure a copy as soon as possible. Are you expected to contact parents by phone or by mail? Will you have conferences with parents on a regular basis?

19. What are the objectives of the school and how do they affect what you will teach?

20. Are you expected to turn in lesson plans? How often? What form is used?

21. Will there be direct supervision? Will someone sit in your class? Will you know in advance? Who will supervise? The principal, rabbi, board member?

22. What adults are permitted in the class? What do you do when an unscheduled visitor arrives?

23. Are student guests allowed in class? Whose responsibility are they? Do you have to accept anyone into your class?

24. Is there a dress code for students? For teacher? What happens when the code isn't followed?

25. How do you physically move students from one part of the school to another? Do they walk in lines or as a group?

26. When students go to art, music, dance, drama, assemblies, and worship services, are you expected to stay with them? Do you participate in these activities? Do you discipline your students or does the enrichment teacher?

27. Are there alternate places on campus where you can take the class for a special story or event?

   Can you answer these questions? Knowing this information will help you on the road to success. The more that you know, the better prepared you will be to teach. You will have confidence. You will know what to do when unexpected situations arise. You will not be dependent upon your students for information or misinformation. *You* will have the power to be in control.

NOTE: Most of these questions are addressed in *Planning for Success* by Dorothy C. Herman, published by Torah Aura Productions. The teacher will find the sections on Discipline, Curriculum, Evaluation, and Substitute Teachers invaluable.

3.
THINGS TEACHERS
NEED TO KNOW

Every teacher has a basic desire to understand what he can do to prepare for success. Long experience has taught that coming to class with a basic idea of curriculum and a day's lesson plan are not enough. A teacher needs to know everything that he can about the school that employs him. He needs to know everything that he can about the children he will teach. He also needs to know everything about himself that will have an effect on the teaching process.

The teacher must plan for success before he goes to the interview for the position. He must know what makes him happy and comfortable in a teaching situation. He must ask the right questions so that he can evaluate whether or not this school is a place where he can experience success. Too many teachers burn out or just become discouraged and never teach again because they choose the wrong environment in which to teach.

I have spent many hours interviewing teachers and working with teachers at workshops in an effort to find out what they want from the teaching experience in a Jewish school. This is what I have discovered.

- Teachers want to feel comfortable in class.
- They want support for curriculum, training, discipline, methodology and problems.

- They want to be creative and to be able to try new things without being in jeopardy of losing their positions.

- They want to know what is expected of them.

- They want solid curriculum and resources.

- They appreciate being able to share with others and to learn from others who have been "through it".

- They want manageable classes (preferably not more than 18 students);

- They want rules that they can follow and that are followed by the administration.

- They want to be involved in decision making where it affects them.

- They want the opportunity to grow.

- They want to be appreciated and recognized.

- They want to have a feeling of belonging.

- They want a professional atmosphere.

- They want administrative and parental support.

- They want a fair salary.

- They want to feel that the time they give will make a difference.

- They want to be successful.

I have also interviewed and worked with students to discover what they want from the Religious School experience and their teachers.

- The students do not want their time wasted. If they have to come to Religious School, they want it to be worthwhile.

- They want a teacher who is knowledgeable. He does not have to know everything, but he should know his particular subject well.

- The teacher should make the class a safe place.

- He should be fair and not have favorites.

- He should never embarrass or yell at a student.

- He should know how to manage a class so that the students know what he wants and are willing to do it.

- The class should be interesting. Students do not want lectures and long readings.

- Religious School should be different from secular school. It should be pleasant and, if possible, fun.

- Students want to be involved. They want to "do something." The teacher should create a different lesson each week. It shouldn't be the same old thing each week and each year.

- Teachers should laugh and enjoy a joke.

- Students like to eat. They appreciate food being built into the curriculum. (Shabbat observances, cookies in the sukkah, latkes for Hanukkah, *hamantashen* for Purim, fruits and nuts on *Tu B'Shevat*, etc.) Note: They do not handle popcorn and potato chips well during educational videos.

- Students want to socialize with their friends as this may be the only time of the week that they see each other.

- Students want teachers to be good role models.

- They want the teacher to care about them. (They appreciate a phone call or a card when they have been out sick for a few sessions.)

- They want to feel successful in the classroom.

As you read this next section, keep the above teacher/student wants in mind. I believe that success comes from preplanning. It doesn't just happen. Each topic and activity has been developed to maximize success. Each was designed to minimize discipline problems by responding to teacher/student needs and wants.

4.
ESTABLISHING
ENVIRONMENTS

As part of my staff development workshop, I ask teachers to step outside the classroom and then to walk back in, look around and really become aware of the classroom environment. I ask them to mentally note the temperature, the lighting, the seating, the bulletin board, the workspaces and flooring. I ask them to become aware of sounds and smells. Then I ask them what the room says to them? Is this a pleasant place to learn? Is it comfortable? Is it conducive to learning? Is it organized? Is it neat and clean? Is there anything Jewish in the room? Does the room have a personality? Does it reflect the teacher's work or the student's work? How can we make it a better Jewish learning environment?

Draw a picture of your classroom including furniture, cabinets, closets, bulletin boards, chalk-boards, chart racks, etc. List your givens (those things that come with the room):

1. Do you share your room with others—day school, preschool, adult education, etc?

2. Do you have storage space? Is it locked? Do you have to share it?

3   Do you have bulletin boards? Do these have to be shared?

4. Is your class the only one in this area during class time or is it a large area with more than one class?

5. Is the furniture age-appropriate?

6. Do you have movable furniture—tables or desks with chairs or chairs with arms?

7. Is there a teacher desk, table or lectern?

8. Is there adequate lighting?

9. Can you control the temperature?

10. Is custodial service available or are you totally responsible for the appearance and set-up of your room?

Total awareness of your environment is necessary if you are to plan for success. The environment will have an effect on discipline and the level of learning.

EXAMPLES:

1. Poor lighting and ventilation will make a child sleepy, inattentive and restless.

2. High level of noise will require techniques for focusing the children's attention on the lesson. The teacher will have to use a different tone or level of voice.

3. Teenagers will feel silly if forced to sit in preschool or primary level chairs.

4. Religious School children will not feel classroom ownership if only day school and preschool materials and work are on the bulletin boards.

5. Attractive nuisances (building blocks, games, art supplies, hanging solar systems) will invite usage and perhaps vandalism. This leads to serious problems for the staff sharing rooms.

A classroom environment should be looked at from every angle. As the teacher, what makes you comfortable? What do you need so that you can be the best you can be?

If it is at all possible, secure furniture that is appropriate for the children that you are teaching. Arrange the room so that it fits your teaching style. If you are fortunate, you will have a custodial staff that will do the arranging for you—if so, consider yourself blessed. If you do not have these necessities, work for change. Discuss the matter with the principal, rabbi, or school board. Change may be slow, but I have found that if you present your case with examples and with ways that it will benefit the students, people will listen and will help. Always show value.

Included here are diagrams that show different furniture arrangements. Each has its advantages and disadvantages. You need to decide which is most comfortable for you.

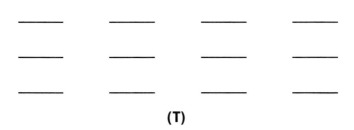

(T)

This arrangement shows the traditional set-up of desks or tables with chairs in straight rows. The teacher's desk is usually placed in the front of the room so that the focus of attention is on her and the chalkboard. Some teachers prefer to place their desks in the rear of the room. With this arrangement there can be movement up and down the aisles. All of the students will face forward. There is little interaction with others. This is a good set-up for children who need structure or who cannot be seated close to others. They are assigned seats or they may choose their places.

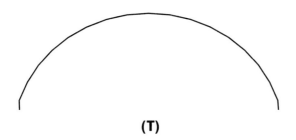

(T)

This semi-circle arrangement is much less formal. It can be set up with chairs only, with desks or small tables, or using chairs with attached armrest desks. It is more conducive to discussions and group interaction than the rows. The teacher can move within the semi-circle or on the outside. It is possible for small groups of students to sit on the floor to work on a project. Students can choose their seats or be assigned. Students who have problems sitting close to one another can be placed at either end of the semi-circle or placed outside of the area for a time-out.

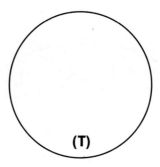

(T)

Clustering is another way to arrange furniture. Students in a cluster of four face each other. This set-up is good for group work and projects. Students can easily interact with their peers and there is space for spreading out materials. The teacher can move easily from cluster to cluster. This set-up is not good if there will be chalkboard work as someone's back will be to the board. One must also be aware that the students will be very close to one another and rules must be firmly established so that excessive talking and kicking under the tables are eliminated.

(T)

This circle arrangement places the teacher as one of the group. It is very informal and gives the participants the feeling of equality. Here the teacher may be more of a facilitator than a formal leader.

Everyone's needs are different. Teenagers in the Religious School may have the need for a more informal setting for the projects and discussions in their curriculum. Younger children need larger work spaces for cutting and pasting. Hebrew classes may need more formal settings for book and written work. The important thing to remember is that awareness of the environment and having it work for you will help the teacher and the students feel successful.

The placement of the teacher's desk is another important decision. Its placement and usage send a message to the students.

EXAMPLE:

(T)

The desk is placed between the chalkboard and the children's desks. If there is a great distance between the two the message will be "Stay back until I ask you to come." How accessible do you want to be? Do you teach from a sitting position behind the desk? Do you sit on top of the desk? Do you use the desk as a barrier to keep the children away from you? Do you get up often and move around the room? Do you have a chair by your desk so that a student can come forward and sit by you for individual help?

Another factor to consider when establishing your environment is seating. Are you comfortable assigning seats? Will you seat the children according to height, boy-girl-boy-girl, boys on one side of the room, girls on the other, or by last names in alphabetical order? Using a seating chart will help the teacher learn the students' names quickly. The teacher will be in control. She can separate cliques of children.

Or would you rather give the students the opportunity to choose their own places? This can be a permanent choice or the child can choose anew each class period. Watch students in this situation. They usually sit in the same seat even when they are not assigned a seat. Sometimes they will assume ownership after sitting in the seat for a few sessions and if someone comes in earlier and sits there they want to know, "Why are you sitting in my seat?"

Students appreciate the opportunity to choose where they will sit. They want to sit near their friends. Sometimes in our Religious Schools children will attend many different secular schools and they look forward to being with a friend that they only see at the week-end or mid-week school. If two students become disruptive when sitting near each other they can be separated without taking freedom of choice away from the other students.

Now, think about your teaching style. What will make *you* comfortable? I have analyzed mine and this is what I have found. I am more at home in an informal setting within a regular classroom. I teach mostly 5th-10th graders or adults. I like movable chairs with armrest desks so that I can rearrange furniture when necessary. I usually want a semi-circle arrangement and I have found myself rearranging furniture when I do teacher training workshops if the seating is in rows. Whenever possible I put in a work order ahead of time. I like the freedom to move around. I find that if two students are chatting too much, I can walk over to them while I am teaching and whisper that I need their cooperation without making a scene and calling undue attention to the students.

I like the informal arrangement so that the students can interact with each other and see the expressions on each other's faces.

I let students sit wherever they please as long as it is within the semi-circle and as long as they do not disrupt the class.

I like a desk in the front of the room so that I have a place to put my materials and books and so that I can do whatever paperwork is necessary. I have learned that I rarely sit behind my desk, but at times I sit or lean upon it. I move around using the chalkboard, bulletin board, media, reading what the students are writing, etc. I know the best environment for me and I try to arrange this whenever possible.

Discover what makes you happy and comfortable. Then do everything that you can to meet this goal. It will have a positive effect on your teaching.

5.
USING LESSON PLANS

There has been much written about lesson plans by a host of experts in the field. This section will not rehash this information. However, I do want to share an exercise that I use in teacher workshops to underline the importance that lesson plans have in the teaching process.

A lesson plan is like a road map. Pretend that you live in Miami and you want to drive to Disney World, which is located in Orlando. You sit down and plan your trip. There are certain 'givens' that you must keep in mind as you plan.

The objective of the trip: Why did you choose to go to Disney World? What do you hope to accomplish by going?

The time available: How long do you want to spend in traveling? How long do you want to spend in Disney World?

Your clients on the trip: Who are you taking with you? What are the ages of the people? Do they have special needs?

Creating interest in the trip: Why do your clients want to go to Disney World? Have they seen pictures or films about the activities there? Have they heard other people tell about their experiences? Can you transmit your excitement about the place and what you will do?

The route you will take: Do you want to go the scenic route or on the turnpike? Do you want to stop along the way for side trips? How many pit stops (bathrooms, food, stretching) will you take?

Activities: What will you do at Disney World? How many attractions will you visit? Will you take several rides of the same type, or will you have a variety of experiences? Will you eat in the park and enjoy shows and music, or will you visit only the main attractions?

Baggage and materials needed: What luggage will you need? What kind of clothes, medicines, etc. will you pack? Will you need toys or games for the children? Do you need to pack a snack? How much money will be needed?

Thinking it over: Did you meet your objective? Did you arrive on time? What happened along the way that was unexpected? Was it worthwhile? Did you have enough of everything that you needed to make the trip comfortable? Would you do it again?

All of these areas of concern and questions are appropriate for a lesson plan also. You need to know where you are going, who you are taking with you, how to create interest in the project, what materials will make it possible for optimal learning to occur and some way to know if you have reached your goal within the time frame that is available.

Many teachers exclaim, "I know what I am doing and where I am going. I just can't write it down. I have planned it out in my head. I've done this lesson many times."

Realize that some teachers may have difficulty with the task of organizing and writing lesson plans. This is especially true of teachers who did not receive formal training through education courses. Your principal will convince you of the necessity of writing lesson plans. Meet with your principal. You may have to verbally explain what you hope to accomplish in the lesson. Your principal can help fill out a lesson plan form using this information, probing for details and clarification and then sharing the results. It will be an easier way to see what is expected in the lesson. As a teacher, you should then complete next week's form with guidance as needed.

Teachers often need to know why the principal requests a lesson plan in advance. Lessons plans are needed:

1. in case of an emergency absence.
2. to ensure that the objectives of that grade level are being met.
3. to check for pacing and the use of varied methodology.
4. to keep special activities and media from being used on two different grade levels so that children will not view Religious School as "the same thing every year."
5. to check that lesson plans can be followed by another teacher or a substitute.
6. to ensure that there is good use of student time.

Pretend that you are a principal, teacher or substitute teacher. You are given the following lesson plans (SAMPLE LESSON PLAN 1 is found on page 27, SAMPLE LESSON PLANS 2 and 3 are found on page 28 and 29). Read the plans carefully. These are actual plans that have been used. Not all of the plans are good. The reader should be critical and determine what is good and what needs to be improved in each one. As you read think about the following. How would you feel about going into a class with this information? What is the teacher trying to accomplish? (OBJECTIVES) Who are his clients? (GRADE LEVEL AND AGE) What directions are given so that you can create interest and enthusiasm for the lesson? (SET INDUCTION) How are you going to accomplish the objectives? (ACTIVITIES) How will you end the session? (CLO-SURE) How can you measure what you have done? (EVALUATION)

Questions to ask the sample lesson plans (pages 27–29):

Do we really know what the objectives are that the teacher will attempt to achieve?

How will the teacher know if the student understands shtetl life?

What does the teacher want the student to know about shtetl life and how will she know if the student has learned anything?

How will the teacher know if the student empathizes with the immigrant?

What does the teacher do to turn the students on to the concepts of the day?

Note that the SET INDUCTION and ACTIVITIES sections are intermingled. How are the students involved in this lesson? Are there enough interesting materials and activities to capture the interest of eighth graders for one and a half hours? Discipline problems occur when there is poor planning. Each step of the lesson plan must be viewed as a road map. Taking everything into consideration, what is the best way to get from point A to point B?

Let's begin again. What does the teacher really want to accomplish?

OBJECTIVES:

At the end of a session the students will:

1. be able to describe a shtetl (location, inhabitants, daily life, religious life, ways to make a living, economy, politics, and dangers).

2. be able to state reasons why Jews left Eastern Europe to settle in America.

3. be able to compare and contrast class members' family immigration experiences.

SET INDUCTION:

Using verbal images, take the class on a journey back in time to the shtetl—a place where many of our grandparents and/or great grandparents lived. Then say, "Let's become observers of this unique community and see if we can better understand the world of our fathers. Look for the following: (items listed in objectives)." Students view the filmstrip and hear the cassette, *Shtetl*.

ACTIVITIES:

Discuss the questions from the teacher's guide to the filmstrip *Shtetl*.

Students will read the first chapter of *My Life*, by Golda Meir. This will focus on one person's experience in the shtetl, its dangers and why her family chose to come to America. Complete questions in workbook. Use these as a basis for discussion.

Review homework assignment (family trees) to compare and contrast students' family immigration experiences. Using the world map, indicate where each family lived originally by placing a flag pin in the area with the family name on the flag. Mark where they settled in America with another flag. List each family's year of immigration. Have the students draw conclusions about when, where, and why this immigration took place then continue with the rest of the worksheet.

CLOSURE:

A formal activity, such as one of the following, will be completed by each student. List three things learned from this lesson; write a paragraph describing life in the shtetl; draw a picture of a shtetl; or write a reaction paragraph about the events in Golda's life.

Read the next two lesson plans. Would you feel comfortable teaching from them? Ask questions similar to those about sample lesson one.

SAMPLE LESSON PLAN 1

TEACHER_____   GRADE _8_   ROOM _____   DATE_____

OBJECTIVES:

1.   Gain understanding of shtetl life

2.   Empathize with Eastern European immigrant

    a.   pogroms

    b.   church

    c.   non-Jews

SET INDUCTION:

1.   Study questions on Golda's life

2.   "My Dovecote"—read and discuss

3.   Comparison of family trees/reports

ACTIVITIES:

1.   Class reports of family trees
    Plotting on map of Europe

2.   Read and discuss 2 articles on Eastern Europe

    a.   Golda—*My Life*

    b.   Babel—"My Dovecote"

3.   Study Questions on Golda

CLOSURE: (including evaluation)

Personal identification of families and self with East European experience

Final understanding between differences of Sephardim, German, East Europeans

SAMPLE LESSON PLAN 2

TEACHER_____   GRADE 2   ROOM _____   DATE_____

OBJECTIVES:

1. The children will be introduced to the holiday of Shabbat through a three-week unit of study.

2. The children will understand the meaning and significance of Shabbat as a day of rest and a special day to give thanks for the blessings and gifts of God.

SET INDUCTION:
Explain how Shabbat is set apart and made special in the home, i.e. best dishes, table-cloths, flowers, special dinner and foods, special prayers and songs, nice clothes and special ways we act.

ACTIVITIES:
1. Ask pivotal questions to stimulate discussion:

   A. Which holiday is celebrated every week throughout the year, 52 each year?

   B. When does Shabbat occur?

   C. When does Shabbat begin and end?

   D. What does Shabbat or Sabbath mean?

   E. How do you celebrate Shabbat in your home?

   F. How do we celebrate Shabbat in our classroom?

2. Begin work in the Shabbat workbook.

3. Cut out Shabbat candlesticks, candles, flame. Paste on construction paper with prayers on the bottom of the page.

4. Teach the blessing over the candles. Have each child recite the blessing. Tell them the English translation.

CLOSURE:
Review the concepts of Shabbat through these Shabbat songs: "This Little Shabbat Light of Mine," "Mothers Gone A Marketing," "Everybody Loves Friday Night," "Bim Bam."

Play the Shabbat Candle Game.

SAMPLE LESSON PLAN 3

TEACHER_____   GRADE <u>6</u>   ROOM _____   DATE_____

OBJECTIVES:

Through the film *Paper Drive* the students will be able to relate what ordinances and commandments were violated.

SET INDUCTION:

Paper Drive and discussion related to the film.

ACTIVITIES:

Paper Drive

The students will be told that they are going to watch a film that is not completed. They will have the opportunity to write the ending. After viewing the film, they will write the ending and then we will discuss the following questions.

   a.   This was an act of *tzedakah.* Do we need material rewards in order to be willing to help others or should we be satisfied by just doing good?

   b.   What ordinances or commandments were violated by the students?

   c.   What was the teacher's problem and how would you have handled it?

   d.   What problems did the children experience and what should they have done?

   e.   Do two wrongs make a right?

   f.   Does one person's cheating justify cheating by others?

   g.   Are there degrees of cheating?

CLOSURE:

Class as a group will write an ending for the story that will reflect knowledge of the ordinances.

Now read the reprint from Griggs, *Teaching Teachers to Teach* (a book for church Religious School teachers). This offers an excellent reference for teachers who need help in writing behavioral objectives. During teacher training workshops I use section F to help teachers become familiar with words that can be used in articulating objectives. Each teacher states an objective using one of the words. For example, the students will *compare* the 10 Commandments in Exodus with those in Deuteronomy. The students will *identify* the symbols found on the Seder plate.

6.
FOCUS ON
INSTRUCTIONAL
OBJECTIVES

Whenever we plan a trip, a special meal, or a project around the house, we usually have specific objectives in mind: to arrive at Lake Tahoe on June 15, to have ten guests for dinner, to be served at 7 p.m., or to finish painting the outside of the house during the two weeks' vacation. It is very easy to evaluate whether or not we achieved these objectives. Obviously, the objectives are not achieved just because we have stated them. It takes much planning to achieve our intended objectives.

Objectives in teaching are somewhat similar. What we want to achieve with the students should be as specific as possible. We should be able to determine at the end of a session or unit of instruction whether or not the objectives for the students have been achieved.

A. First, some words of definition:

1. **Objective**, noun. "An aim or end of action; point to be hit, reached, etc."(*Webster's New Collegiate Dictionary*)

2. **Objective**. "A collection of words describing a teacher's intent for the student." (Robert F. Mager)

3. **"Behavioral objectives** are statements which describe what students will be able to do after completing a prescribed unit of instruction." (Kibler, Barker, and Miles)

B. COMPARE GOALS WITH OBJECTIVES:

All church school curriculum is written with goals stated someplace in the introduction or other appropriate place. As teachers we usually have some in mind that we can state if someone asks us. Many times teachers use goals and objectives as synonymous. I think it is very important to distinguish the differences between goals and objectives. On the next page you will see a chart which is an attempt to summarize those differences.

C. Next, the **criteria for writing** instructional objectives:

1. An objective should be written in terms of **student** performance. Does it say what we expect of the student?

2. An objective should state in **observable** terms what students will be expected **to do**. Does it describe something we can **see** or **hear** the students do?

3. An objective should be **specific**. Does it describe clearly and specifically what is expected of the student?

4. An objective should state something of the **conditions** within which the student will be expected to perform. Does it indicate the condition that will influence a student's action?

5. An objective should be **measurable**. Does it include a statement of quality or level of intended performance?

6. An objective should be **sequential** in relation to previous and following objectives. Does it relate in sequence to what preceded and what is to follow?

D. Start writing an objective with the following statement:

"At the end of the session(s) the students should be able to:"

Note: *This is a very helpful way to begin every instructional objective. It focuses on the* **student** *and what the teacher intends for him to be able to* **do**.

COMPARING GOALS AND OBJECTIVES

GOALS...are big enough to spend a whole life-time pursuing.

...are beyond our reach; we will never fully achieve the goals of Christian living.

...give us direction for our teaching, learning, relating, deciding, etc.

...are too general to use for planning and evaluating teaching activities.

A person's growing toward a goal is influenced by many factors beyond the sphere of influence of the teacher.

A GOAL

"Persons will become more loving and caring toward other persons."

(sample)

THE CLASSROOM

Learning activities and resources.

OBJECTIVES...are specific.

...are written in terms of what students can be expected to accomplish, in particular learning activities.

...are achievable.

...are just little steps along the way toward the larger goal.

...are very helpful guidelines for teachers to use in planning and evaluating teaching activities.

...A person's achievement of objectives is directly influenced by the work of the teacher.

Objective

"At the end of the period of study, the students will be able to visit an elderly person of the church to share a gift and conversation with that person."

(sample)

E. After the introductory statement the next word is the key to the whole objective.

At the end of the session(s) the students should be able to:

understand ....

know ....

believe ....

realize ....

appreciate ....

feel ....

acknowledge ....

Note: *These words are too general. These are goal-orientated words. They do not help teachers determine whether students have accomplished what was intended. There is nothing wrong with "understanding," etc., per se, but as guidelines in planning for and evaluating teaching they are not very helpful.*

F. At the end of the session(s) the students should be able to:

demonstrate	list	cite
compare	describe	follow
identify	show	quote
state	organize	name
create	write	summarize
explain	express	contribute
present	suggest	participate
apply	locate	select
find	discuss	ask

Note: *All of the above words are actions students can do which can be* **seen** *or* **heard** *by teachers. Such actions by students provide clues to the teacher that enable the teacher to evaluate more objectively whether or not students have achieved what teachers intended.*

AN ACTIVITY TO PRACTICE WRITING INSTRUCTIONAL OBJECTIVES

STEP ONE—Compare two statements

Read the following two statements and compare the differences between them.

1. The purpose of the class period should be to be able to use a Bible Concordance.

2. At the end of the session the students should be able to use a Bible Concordance to find five familiar passages of scripture related to the concept "covenant."

Some questions to consider:

What differences have you identified?

Which statement is more general than the other?

Which statement is more directed to student activity?

Which statement would be more helpful after the session to guide the teacher in evaluating whether or not the objective was achieved?

Statement two (2) is the better of the two because it is more specific, more focused on student activity, and more helpful for later evaluation.

STEP TWO—Compare two more statements

Read the following two statements and compare them.

1. At the end of the session the students should be able to **list** six different actions and/or teachings of both Amos and Jeremiah and to **compare** the differences and similarities between them.

2. At the end of the session the students should be able to **understand** some of the important teachings of the prophets Amos and Jeremiah.

Some questions to consider:

What do you notice about these two statements when you compare them?

Which objective states actions of the students that can be seen or heard?

Which objectives would be more helpful in evaluating the students' achievements?

The first (1) statement is the better of the two because it states in observable terms what a student is expected to do.

A Summary Statement

The above two sets of examples of objectives focus on the two primary, essential criteria for writing objectives; (1) written for students in terms of their action and (2) written with students actions that can be observed—we can see and/or hear what the students do. Whenever writing objectives these two elements should always be included.

There are two other criteria which help make objectives more specific and achievable: the **conditions** under which they will be achieved and the **quality** of achievement expected by the teacher. These two aspects of objectives will sharpen them, but may not be included in every objective a teacher writes.

STEP THREE—Two Additional Criteria Objectives

A.   The conditions under which objectives will be achieved include time, materials, resources, and in the following objectives **conditions** are printed in **bold**.

    1.   By using a **Bible Dictionary** and **commentary (given 30 minutes time)** students should be able to write a two-paragraph interpretation of Psalm 23 in their own words.

    2.   Given an **unlabeled map** of the lands of the Bible, the students should be able to locate accurately all the following places: Dead Sea, Jordan River, Egypt, Sea of Galilee and the Sinai Peninsula.

B.   The **quality** with which objectives will be achieved says something of the level of expectation that a teacher has. In the following objectives the words which indicate **quality** are printed in **bold.**

    1.   By using a Bible dictionary and commentary (given 30 minutes time) the students should be able to write a **two-paragraph** interpretation of Psalm 23 **in their own words.**

    2.   Given an unlabeled map of the lands of the Bible the students should be able to locate **accurately all** the following places....

7.
USING TEACHER-MADE WORKBOOKS

Many times during the course of the year, a teacher will create a worksheet to use with a lesson. It may be questions to answer at the end of a chapter or film, a study guide to use while reading or a game to use after an oral exercise. These dittos or photocopied papers are done in school or for homework, are checked by the teacher or by other students, and then are given back to the students and tossed out or maybe the teacher will do the tossing.

There is an effective alternative for these worksheets. After the course has been taught at least once or maybe a few times, gather together all of the worksheets. Look them over carefully. Redo them if needed. Organize them in the order of the course. Put a picture or graphic on the cover. (Our class on Comparative Religion had a contest to create a cover. The winning entry was used for two years.) Write an introductory page—a letter from the teacher—and a table of contents. Number each page. Include course material in addition to the worksheets. Duplicate class copies of your new workbook. Always remember that the workbook is not chiseled in stone. Review the material at the end of the course. Remove worksheets that no longer apply. Add new pages as you become more creative with your course.

Using the teacher-made workbook has had a profound effect upon my teaching and upon my students.

When the students come into class they soon realize that the teacher is very well organized. He knows where he in going. He is not coming in to "wing it."

The students are given their workbooks. They put their names on them. Each week when they come to class the workbooks are on the teacher's desk. They soon fall into the habit of picking them up and taking them to their desks. The workbooks are collected at the end of each class, reviewed by the teacher during the week, and are evaluated or subject to comments. The workbooks are sent home the session before tests are given so that the students may study. NOTE: *We do not assign homework unless a student has excessive absences. Experience has taught us that due to secular school and after-school pressures, the assignments are not completed. There is no guarantee that the workbooks would be returned the following week if they went home after each class. Therefore, each lesson is self contained and all work is completed in class.*

The students need to bring a pencil or pen to class each week. The paper they will need is in the workbook.

The teacher can see who is having a problem with the curriculum and he can work with those students. He can also see at a glance which concepts are difficult for all of the students so that he can reteach sections that came across as fuzzy.

Every student must **do** something each session. It is very easy for the quiet or disinterested student to sit in class and do nothing. Usually there are a few vocal superstars in each class. The teacher may think that there are great discussions and tremendous learning happening, when in reality only a few students are participating. Writing is a way of involving everyone. Sometimes it is good to have everyone in class respond to a question, the media, the text, in writing, and then open the floor to discussion.

The workbook is very helpful for students who have been absent. Background material and the page in the workbook can be duplicated and sent to the student or he can complete it when he returns. The message is sent that the material covered in class is very important and when you miss class, you miss something special. It also says that the student must be responsible for the work.

The workbook provides the opportunity for added communication between student and teacher. The students can be encouraged to write comments about the class and the lesson, things that were good or things that made them uncomfortable. The teacher can comment on the work, the student's behavior and participation, and the student's communication. Comments have ranged from, "Hi, Mrs. Herman. I hope that you are having a good night." to "I find it difficult to discuss death rituals in class. My grandmother died last week."

Each semester I ask my students to comment on the usefulness of the workbook. Overwhelmingly the response is positive.

At this time workbooks have been developed throughout the school. In the primary grades, the pages are filled with puzzles and games as well as questions. Sometimes there is a holiday workbook that is sent home at the end of a unit. Materials for parents are included so that they can help the family observe the holiday at home (background material, blessings, recipes, games). The teachers who use these workbooks love them. They create their own workbooks individually or as a grade level. They change from year to year and when new teachers join us. New teachers are grateful for the materials that are already prepared and for the organization that is provided. When I do workshops around the country and share the workbooks from all the classes, the teachers want to know if they can have copies. I tell them that these were prepared for our situation and our classes. They must take the idea and create their own. Try it. It is a wonderful tool.

8.
BUILDING COMMUNITY
IN THE CLASSROOM

One of the major reasons parents have for sending their children to Religious School is so that they will meet and become friendly with other Jewish children. While there are still many "Jewish neighborhoods," more of our students live in very mixed areas and the temple may be the only place and Religious School the only time that they are with other Jewish children. This is especially true of city or scattered suburban neighborhoods. For example, we have 101 students in our seventh grade. These students attend at least ten different secular schools during the week. The parents look to the Religious School as the place where the students will meet others to invite to their bar and bat mitzvah ceremonies and to socialize with on the weekends.

At times this is not a reasonable expectation for the school as the students spend so little time there. It is important for the temple to recognize this need by providing other activities that would involve the students: youth group, cotillion, sports, student services, retreats, family dinners, singing groups, etc.

The school should also address this need within the classroom. Children need a sense of belonging to the temple and to a people. They need to know that others their own age celebrate the same holidays and participate in the same life cycle events. Sharing a common heritage fosters the feeling that the student's family is not the only one who does certain Jewish things, but that we as a people have things in common with each other. We should encourage our students to socialize with each other so that they feel comfortable and at home with each other. If a child has even one friend in class, coming to Religious School will be a more pleasant experience. Many years down the road, we hope the child will date others from the temple and will seek out those with similar beliefs and experiences when thinking about marriage.

Students in the Religious School should have many opportunities to work together in both large and small groups. They should work on reports, committees, and projects that will give them a vehicle to share ideas and feelings. When students are involved and have mutual goals, friendships can form. They can learn from each other and appreciate each others' talents. Religious School and, by extension, the temple will become a friendlier place to them because they will feel more at home. If it is agreeable to the parents, class lists with phone numbers and addresses can be distributed so that the students can continue these friendships outside of class.

The classroom should be a place in which the students can share their feelings and problems in a no-risk atmosphere. Ground rules should be established at the beginning of the year. We help each other feel successful. Everyone has strong points and weak points. We will accept each other as we are and we will help each other to grow.

Keeping these thoughts in mind, the teacher can structure the class for this socialization. Beginning the first day of school the teacher can introduce activities so that the students can become acquainted with each other and can begin to interact with each other.

The following activities have been used successfully throughout our school. Use them as written or adapt them to your own situation.

LET'S GET TO KNOW EACH OTHER

This activity is a good icebreaker for the first day of school. The students will have the opportunity to meet and discuss a topic with one partner and will then become acquainted with everyone in the class. Judaic symbols are used to move the students attention from the secular world and to help them focus on the Jewish world.

Each student is given one half of a two-piece puzzle. The puzzle picture can be sketched and colored or it can be from a book. It is placed on a five by seven inch index card. Puzzle pieces can include: Ten Commandments, Torah, sukkah, shofar, matzah, menorah, Shabbat candles, kiddush cup, *gragger* and masks, tree.

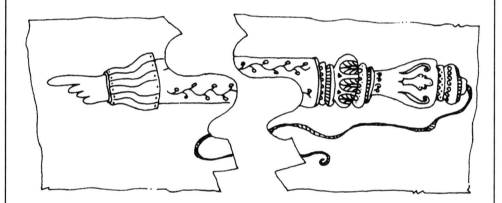

The students are instructed to
1. move around the room and find the person holding the other half of your puzzle.
2. introduce yourself to this person.
3. sit together with this person and together identify the symbol and be able to tell the class its name, use and holiday associated with it.
4. in five minutes find out about this person (name, school, hobby, summer activities, best and worst school subjects, ambitions etc.).
5. Each pair will then introduce each other to the group and tell as much as they can about the other person. They also share their puzzle and its significance.

From *Experimental Methodology In Teaching Training*, By Dorothy C. Herman

CLASSROOM BINGO

Each student is given a blank Bingo worksheet. They are asked to walk around the room and to learn the names of the other students. They write the students' names in the squares, repeating some if necessary to fill all of the boxes. The teacher places each name on a card and puts it into a container. She picks a name from the container and calls it out. Students look for the name on their sheet and mark it. Play continues until someone has five marks in a row and calls out "Bingo." Names are checked against those that have been called. The student can then be asked to match the name to the student.

Suzanne	Jason	Marci	Adam	Richard
Alison	Melanie	Debi	Greg	Jeff
Jessie	Risa	Brooke	Hilary	Yael
Stuart	Avi	Mindy	Sarah	Benji
Jack	Amy	Jessica	Jill	Ari

Sample of Classroom Bingo

JUST LIKE ME

Name _____

Students are each given a worksheet and a pencil. They are instructed to move around the room and to talk to as many of their classmates as they can, asking them questions that respond to the categories listed. If they match, the student writes the classmate's name in the appropriate box.

At Beth Am Religious School the same number of years	Attends the same weekday school	Born in the same city	Has the same number of people in family
Has the same hobby	Has the same favorite color	Has the same Zodiac sign	Has the same shoe size
Is wearing the same color shoes	First name begins with the same letter	Has the same favorite animal	Has the same feelings about Religious School

Sample of Just Like Me

This is an excellent way to help students become acquainted with each other. Four or five minutes later, the students return to their desks and as a group they can share answers.

This exercise can also be used with curricular materials in the boxes. For example: Your favorite commandment. Find someone else who shares it. What do you like to do on Shabbat? A favorite holiday food. etc....

PROBLEM BOX

Students can help each other by sharing and solving problems together. The Problem Box is an example of how this can work. A shoebox is labelled Problem Box and is placed on a shelf in the room. The teacher tells about using the box by sharing a problem that she may have. She then asks the children to think about the problem and to give her advice as to how she can solve it. The students will involve themselves in the problem and will work towards solutions that they think will really help. The suggestions are listed on the board and are then discussed as to the consequences of following the advice given. The teacher decides which suggestions she thinks will be helpful and tells the children that she will try them. She may also give feedback the following week so that the children will see how she fared.

The problem can deal with something at school or at home. For example, my neighbor has two dogs that roam the neighborhood, knocking over trash cans. The dogs come close to my screened-in patio which annoys my big Doberman. My dog barks continually and has even broken through the screening. I then have to run after the dogs and bring mine back. I have asked my neighbor to keep her dogs in her fenced-in yard as our county has a leash law which states that a dog may not be off the owner's property without a leash. She says that the dogs keep getting out and that she is sorry, but she is not correcting the situation. What should I do? I don't want to fight with my neighbor, but my dog and my house are suffering. Do I have to lock up my dog? Should I call the dog pound and have them pick up her dogs? Should I continue talking to her? What should I do? I do not want to make her my enemy.

The students discuss the problem. They become annoyed with the neighbor also and can make some very strong suggestions. All suggestions are written down and discussed. The most viable solutions will be tried and the results reported to the group.

The students begin to realize that everyone can have a problem and that we can receive help from our classmates and friends. The teacher shows the class the Problem Box and asks them to think about a problem that they may have. It can be with teachers, other students, parents, siblings or friends. The students are encouraged to write about their problem on a 3" x 5" card and to place it in the Problem Box. The card should be unsigned so that no one knows whose problem is listed. Each week a problem or two will be chosen and discussed, and solutions will be offered. New problems may be added whenever someone wants to put one in the box.

Over the years we have discussed many different kinds of problems: curfews, fights between friends and siblings, being picked on by others, doing poorly in school, unfair teachers, fear of failure, peer pressure, drugs, and having a Christmas tree in our home. The students take the problems seriously and really try to help each other. Sometimes students put in cards saying how they finally resolved the problem. Usually before the year is over trust is built within the class, students bypass the cards and only share, "I have a problem and I need help." How wonderful if Religious School students can feel this close that they can come to each other for help!

PLANNING CLASS EVENTS

Planning parties or events can also help bring students closer together. For example, the traditional school Seder can become more meaningful if the students are in charge of its success. Not only will the class be totally involved and "own" it, but community will build within the class as the students work together for the common good.

The Seder can take place in the school or in someone's home. Moving the event off campus makes the day even more special. Committees are listed and students choose their job in advance.

RITUAL COMMITTEE:

This group works with the Haggadah. Together with the teacher or alone if they are able, they look through the Haggadah, mark off the parts that will be included, assign reading and explanatory parts to members of the committee and others, and then read through the text to insure that they are familiar with the correct pronunciation. The committee is responsible for setting the mood for the experience. Someone may want to begin with a sharing of her home Seder experience or a meaningful experience at a Seder that she remembers fondly. A student may want to read a poem or play music to set the mood. Students may be called upon to share "What Passover means to me." Let them enjoy being creative.

ART COMMITTEE:

The students in this group are responsible for giving the area a festive atmosphere. The students can create posters, place mats or centerpieces with a Passover theme. Art materials must be supplied. If there is an art teacher at the school she can be consulted and if possible be available to help. Our fifth and sixth-grade students who participate at a "kibbutz Seder" as part of our Touring Israel curriculum made flags representing their kibbutz. They have also created wonderful peace posters.

FOOD COMMITTEE:

This group consults the Haggadah for ritual foods that must be included and then adds appropriate additional items. They decide how much is needed to feed the total class. They also decide if they will collect money and shop for the food or assign items to be brought in by each student. Assigning items is usually the least complicated approach. The committee can give each student a form that states what they will bring. They may want to follow through with a telephone call to each student a few days before the Seder to remind them of their obligation. These students may also check the food as it comes in and decide what to do if there are shortages. They set the food out for the next committee.

FOOD PREPARERS:

This group will chop the nuts and apples for the *haroset*. They will open the cans of gefilte fish and place the fish on plates so that the servers can put them on the table. They will pour the grape juice.

TABLE SETTERS:

This group is responsible for setting the tables. They are provided with a list of the items that need to be on the table and on each plate.

SERVERS:

During the Seder this group will refill grape juice glasses and matzah plates.

CLEAN UP:

When the Seder has ended, this group remains behind to clear the tables, package leftover food, and insure that kiddush cups, candlesticks, Seder plates and other special dishes from home are returned to the owners.

The committees must know what they are expected to do. Depending upon class size, students may be members of more than one committee. The students must have the proper tools and directions so that they can be successful.

The teachers and helping parents act as guides. They do not do the work. They answer questions and perhaps make suggestions, but the students are the workers. If something spills, the students handle it. If there is not enough of an item, the students find solutions. Upon completion of an activity, the teacher should make positive comments and should help the students realize what has been accomplished. The students will be proud of themselves and their committee.

For other successful models, see the following:

> *Touring Israel, From Generation to Generation,* and *The Joy of Shabbat* all written by the author and published by the Central Agency for Jewish Education, Miami, Florida. These curricula were designed for maximum interaction amongst the students.

WELCOMING THE NEW STUDENT

Throughout the year, new students enroll in the school. Many will begin the first day of school while others will join in the middle of the year. Whenever it occurs, the teacher must be aware that this new child feels strange and not connected. It is important for the teacher to take the time to help the child feel wanted and a part of the class. The child should be introduced to the class, should tell a little about herself, should learn a little about the school and class, and should be assigned a buddy. The buddy should introduce the student to others, show her where things are in the classroom, and help her find her way around the school.

Example: Six weeks into the school year a new student joins the alef class in the Hebrew department. The child is nervous as she has to adjust to a new neighborhood, a new secular school and now a class with a foreign language. The principal brings the child to the room and introduces her to the teacher and class and then leaves. The teacher says, "Welcome to our class. Hebrew may seem a little strange at first, but I know that you will catch on. Today we will be learning some new letters and reviewing what we already know. We will all help you and soon you will be caught up with the class. Sit with Jenny so that she can be your buddy.

After class the teacher should spend a few minutes with the newcomer and tell her why we learn Hebrew. She should encourage her to share her reactions to the class and the lesson. She can begin allaying any fears she may have. Arrangements should be made to help the child make up the necessary work to catch up with the class. It is the teacher's job to help each child feel welcome and wanted.

QUESTIONNAIRE TO LEARN ABOUT EACH CHILD

The following worksheet (page 50) can be given to the class at the end of the first class session. The teacher has already set the tone for a successful year. The students should feel comfortable in this new situation. The teacher explains that she really wants to know how to help each child do his or her best and that she would like them to fill out the worksheet so that she can meet this goal.

The students are usually very honest when filling out this form. They are happy to give information that will insure their success. The teacher can learn many things about the class and the individuals in it. If most of the class responds that they learn best by one particular approach, the wise teacher will include many opportunities for them to use it. If the students favor many different approaches the teacher will need to plan activities using varied methodology.

QUESTIONNAIRE TO LEARN ABOUT EACH CHILD

Name_____

Rank order your choices: 1 is your first choice, 6 is your last choice

1. I learn best by:
    _____reading (books–material)
    _____hearing (lectures–discussions)
    _____seeing (observing)
    _____using media (videos, films, filmstrips)
    _____doing (experiencing–using my hands)
    _____Other: describe _____

2. (√) which applies to you
    _____I am an excellent reader
    _____I am a good reader
    _____I am a fair reader
    _____I am a poor reader

3. I learn best in
    _____large groups
    _____small groups
    _____by myself

4. I am
    _____right handed
    _____left handed
    _____use both hands equally

5. I learn best if I am seated
    _____closest to the front of the room
    _____furthest away from the front of the room
    _____in the middle of the room
    _____I can sit anywhere

6. List anything that the teacher should know so that you will have a good learning experience. _____
    _____

NOTE: I *have used this worksheet in many teacher training workshops. I list each learning approach on the chalkboard and list the teacher's name under her first two choices. They are always surprised to see the wide range of choices. We then discuss the need for varied methodology. A typical Religious School lesson may have three objectives for the morning. The wise teacher will use five or six different approaches to achieve them. This could include a film, discussion, worksheet, drawing of the main idea, role playing etc. Chances are good that at least one of these varied methods will reach each child.*

It is important to know about the reading skills of a class. We do not have time to test for these skills. The students' answers can indicate how much reading we can expect them to do and still feel successful in class. A group of poor or fair readers cannot be expected to feel good in a text oriented class.

It is helpful to know which students prefer to work alone or in groups. The teacher can organize the lesson and assignments along those lines and find ways to include all children in some group activities.

The question on right/left-handedness will indicate if the teacher needs a supply of left-handed scissors and chairs with left arm desks.

Some children, because of poor eyesight, hearing, or attention deficits, need permanently assigned front row seats. Children will usually indicate a need to sit in a specific area if they are asked.

Children will also tell you things you would never find out if you didn't ask. We have had students tell us that they go to special schools, that they read poorly and do not want to be asked to read out loud, that they have a new baby brother, that they want to sit away from another child because they get into trouble together, that their parents are getting divorced, that they are allergic to chocolate etc... All of this information can be very important to the teacher.

9.
USING INDIVIDUAL OR GROUP RESEARCH

S tudent research work can add an extra dimension to your class. It is a positive way to cover a wide range of materials in a short period of time. Instead of everyone studying the same subject, individuals or small groups can research particular subjects and then creatively share their findings with the rest of the class. The following procedures will give this activity a structure that will help insure its success as a learning experience.

CHOOSE A TOPIC: Famous American Jews—Their Contribution to the United States and the world.

LIST YOUR OBJECTIVES

1. The students will do research and prepare an oral report for the class on a particular famous American Jew using a visual aid.

2. The students will take notes on each other's presentations.

3. The students will be able to identify at least three famous American Jews from each stated category (Religion, politics, sports, entertainment, music, business/labor, literature, etc.).

4. The students will be able to write at least three sentences describing the contributions of these people to the United States and the world (in notebook or on final exam).

5. The students will be able to write a paragraph describing the Jewish contribution to at least three of the stated fields studied (in a notebook or on a final exam).

6. The students will evaluate each other's contributions to their knowledge.

7. Ideally, the students will take pride in the Jewish contribution to America and will try to emulate these people as they grow older.

PROCEDURE:

1. Motivate the students by creating a need to know more about American Jewish contributions to the United States and the world. Ask the students to number their papers from one to ten on both sides. On one side have the students list ten famous Americans. Ask each student to read his list. The teacher writes each name on the chalkboard, creating categories of politics, music entertainment etc. into which they fit. The class can discuss where most of the names were listed, how we know about these people, and why it was so easy to name ten famous Americans.

    On the other side of the paper ask the students to list ten famous American Jews. Again each student reads his list and the famous people are added to the categories on the chalkboard. Discussion again follows as to where we placed most of the people, how we know about them and why it was difficult for most of the class to name 10 people. (It usually is.)

2. Read the section "It happened only once in History" from Max Dimont's book *Jews, God, And History*. In this book, Dimont writes about the small number of Jews in the total world population and their tremendous impact on the world. He states that 12% of all of the Nobel prize winners have been Jews and he lists the various fields in which the contributions were made. He speaks about the lasting effect of the Jewish people compared to others who were on the scene in ancient days, and of how other faiths emerged from the Jewish religion.

    Discuss the following with the class:
    If this statement is correct then why do we not know more about the Jewish contribution to the world? In public school we learn about the contributions and life of George Washington and other presidents, of Eli Whitney and other heroes of the Industrial Revolution, of Martin Luther King Jr. and other black notables, but we do not learn about what the Jews did to make America great. This unit of study will help us see that the Jewish people have indeed contributed to all aspects of the American culture.

3. A bulletin board may be used to reinforce the motivation. Use symbols of the categories and pictures of Famous American Jews on a bulletin board with headings "Do you know

54

why these people are famous?" or "What do you know about the contributions of Jews to America and the world?"

4. Prepare the foundation for research work by indicating that there are many areas where Jewish people have made major contributions to our society. We do not have time for each of us to read about all of these people. Therefore, we will help each other by doing our part and then by sharing with the others.

    a. The teacher writes a number for each student on a small square of paper and puts these in a box. Each student then picks a number. The teacher calls the numbers in order. The student comes forward and writes his name on the chalkboard under the category that interests him (see number three in *objectives*). At the end of the choosing, students may exchange categories if someone wants to change. (This gives friends the opportunity to work together unless the teacher feels that a particular group would benefit from not working together.) Once this is completed, no changes may occur.

NOTE: *Using the number system, the teacher is impartial as to which child gets which report. It is done by chance and is fair for all. This technique lessens discipline problems within the class.*

    b. Students are given guide sheets. Each writes the name of his committee on the paper. See Example 1, page 60.

    c. The teacher should then ask about dates the students know that they will be absent (bar/bat mitzvah, trips etc.) NOTE: These are reality and should be taken into consideration as you plan for success.

        Assign dates for the report emphasizing the need for the committee to work together and to be prepared on time.

    d. Have the students form committee groups and list their committee members and phone numbers. Give each group a list of the famous people in their category and a bibliography. Give them time to plan and choose a famous person. Have books and materials available so that they can begin research at this time. At the end of the first session they should each have chosen their famous person and have begun their research work.

    e. The students should have at least two more research periods during class. Some of them may want to work at home, but usually Religious School students do not welcome additional assignments "on their time."

f. A special time should be allotted for creating a visual aid. At this time art supplies should be available. If there is an art teacher on staff you may want to plan with him or have him visit the class during this time.

NOTE: *Students at our school have also added to their reports by creating games (To Tell the Truth, Who Am I), dramatizing an event in their famous person's life, playing music that their person wrote using cassettes or playing the piano or guitar, videotaping segments from television that are appropriate, showing pictures from books on an opaque projector and using parts of filmstrips that are in our teacher center.*

5. Presentations should follow the procedures as outlined on the guide sheet.

   a. The whole committee should come forward for the presentation. One member should write the name of the topic category on the chalkboard. Each person should write the name of his famous person as he does his report.

   b. When the group completes the presentation, questions about the report are directed to the class by the presenting committee. (The class must listen actively so that they will know the answers.)

   c. The class should take notes during the presentation, answer questions, and then be able to ask questions of the presenting group. (The audience members cannot dis-associate themselves from the lesson. They have a specific assignment. They know what is expected of them. They must be involved.)

   d. The teacher should be prepared to add information that is not covered in the student report. Students not in the group may also have additional information. It is important that inaccurate information be corrected. If an inaccurate statement is made and is not corrected then the class will assume that it is true and wrong information will be processed. Sometimes teachers are afraid to correct a statement made by a student as they do not wish to cause him embarrassment, but this can be done in a positive way.

   e. The teacher then asks the students to comment on the reports using the following rules as a guide.

      Find something positive to say about another's work. Don't use generalities. For example: "He did a fine job." This really does not say anything. The teacher asks, "What was good about the report? What part was really meaningful?" For example: "The chart was very clear." "The committee was well prepared." "The facts about the person were interesting."

      When commenting on something negative, make it constructive. For example: "The charts would have been more effective if the print was larger" is better than "The chart was terrible." "I would have liked to have known more about his contributions" is better than "You really didn't tell us anything about him."

The students will fill out an evaluation form (See Example 2, page 61) on each committee member. The teacher collects these and then writes her own evaluation (See Example 3, page 62). The teacher will read the evaluations during the week and write an evaluation for each student based on the class-mates' observations and her own.

NOTE: *Throughout the assignment the students always knew what was expected of them individually and as a group. Each step was planned to insure the success of the activity. There was total involvement on the part of the students. They were required to:*

A. Follow directions

B.   Work with a group

C. Complete research

D.   Prepare a visual aid

E. Prepare questions

F.   Present an oral report

G. Take notes while listening to reports

H.   Answer questions

I.   Evaluate reports

Think back to the many research projects and oral reports that you have seen and heard. Usually the only persons involved during the oral report are the reporter and the teacher. When nothing is required of the students in the audience, they can doodle, let their minds wander, talk to their neighbors etc. Detailed planning for each member of the class will prevent this.

GUIDELINES FOR REPORTS ON AMERICAN JEWISH HISTORY

1. Students will work as a group on:

   a. General contributions to a particular field.

   b. A presentation for the class which will include a visual display.

   c. Review questions for class after presentation.

2. Students will each work individually on one person from the chosen field and will write a report that will include:

   a. General background of person (name, birth, death, childhood background, education).

   b. The outstanding contribution that this person has made to the United States or the world.

   c. The Jewish influence on his/her life.

   d. What you admire about this person.

3. On the day of the presentation, all students will take notes on each other's reports and will be able to answer key questions asked by participants.

4. All students will evaluate each other's reports using the following criteria:

   a. Was the committee prepared?

   b. Did each participant give an in-depth report?

   c. Did the visual aid contribute to the report?

   D. What did you learn that you didn't already know?

My committee is: _____

Other committee members and phone numbers:_____

_____

My important personality is:_____

The date our report is due:_____

Example 1

EXAMPLE OF STUDENT EVALUATION FORM

YOUR NAME _____

SUBJECT OF REPORT_____

REPORTER (S)_____

Please rate the following using the key listed below.

	EXCELLENT	GOOD	FAIR	NEEDS IMPROVEMENT
Committee Preparation	❏	❏	❏	❏
Oral Report:	❏	❏	❏	❏
Visual Aid	❏	❏	❏	❏
Questions	❏	❏	❏	❏

I learned_____

Comments_____

_____

Example 2

EXAMPLE OF TEACHER EVALUATION FORM

STUDENT NAME(S) _____

_____

TEACHER'S COMMENT—

 Your classmates enjoyed your report on Emma Lazarus. Your visual aid was helpful as they could read her poem and see where it is found. This will help them to remember her and her contribution. They suggest that you speak more slowly so that they can take better notes. I agree with their comments. I also thought that your information was very interesting. You appeared to enjoy your topic and working with your committee.

I thought your report was _____

	EXCELLENT	GOOD	FAIR	NEEDS IMPROVEMENT
Oral Report:	❑	❑	❑	❑
Visual Aid	❑	❑	❑	❑
Questions	❑	❑	❑	❑

Example 1

10.
USING GAMES

Games can be an excellent tool for introducing new material, reviewing learned concepts, and preparing for tests. Games are enjoyable for the student and provide a change of pace in the classroom. The inclusion of games in the curriculum necessitates prior planning. Use a regular lesson plan when preparing for gaming.

Games can be used in small groups within the classroom, with the total class or even with larger groups. Successful gaming is the outcome of successful planning.

The following illustrates successful planning. Each game presented can be used in an individual classroom. The overall plan can be used for any large group, total school, or camp weekend.

For a number of years we have had our annual Hanukkah Game Day for our entire seventh and eighth grades. The junior high students need to feel a separation from the elementary grades. This activity takes the place of individual classroom Hanukkah parties that the younger students enjoy.

OBJECTIVES

1. The students will play familiar television games using Judaic materials that will reflect the curriculum of the fourth through seventh grades.
2. The students will work in teams and will socialize with students from the six classes in the junior high department.
3. The students will share the holiday of Hanukkah in an enjoyable way.
4. The students will eat Hanukkah foods, sing Hanukkah songs and blessings.

PROCEDURE:

The idea for a Hanukkah Game Day was presented to the seventh and eighth-grade teachers as an alternative to the usual Hanukkah parties. They enthusiastically agreed to try it.

1. The teachers met for a gaming workshop. Rules for each game were taught. Each game was played through to completion and was then analyzed as to problems that might occur, techniques used, and materials needed. Each teacher chose the game that she would lead at the game day. Rules and descriptions of each game and the master plan for the day were distributed.

2. One week before the game day the students were told that because they were in the Junior High Department, their Hanukkah parties would be different. The students would have the opportunity to be with their friends from the other classes for a very special gaming day. The students were told about the games and were motivated to look forward to the following week.

3. The students were asked to volunteer to bring in refreshments for the party. These included latkes, applesauce, soda, general noshes, and jelly doughnuts. One student was asked to supply a menorah. The school would supply all paper goods, chocolate gelt, dreidels, candles and matches.

4. Each class had a list of two or three parents who volunteered to help with the parties. The teacher called the parents and explained the day to them. The parents would be responsible for setting up the refreshments table, "guarding" the food during the gaming period, and serving at the end of the morning. If needed, they could help with the games.

5. On "the day" the teachers reported to the gaming area (our gym—any large room will do) one half hour before school started. At this time they set up their gaming areas, organized their games and props. Each station would also have pencils and a pad of paper to record the scores.

6. Ten minutes after class began two students from each class brought the refreshments to the leader in the gym. They remained to help the room parents organize the food according to category (drinks, cookies, applesauce, donuts, fruit, paper goods, dreidels, gelt etc.). They acted as runners bringing latkes to the warming ovens and ice to the gym. They also brought a head count from their class so that we would know exactly how many students would be involved.

NOTE: *We usually have 90 to 110 students, six to eight teachers, an administrative assistant and myself.*

7. The activity began one half hour after school started. Each teacher led her class to the gym. (It is important for the teacher to be at the head of the line so that classes can be controlled and separated from each other.) As the students entered the gym they received

numbered name tags. Five students would be on a team. The tags were purposely mixed up so that teams would be made up of students from both grade levels and from different classes. Trash cans were available for the name tag backs. The students sat on the floor in the middle of the room. The teacher reviewed the above procedure with the students while they were in the classroom so that they would know what was expected of them.

8. When all of the groups were seated the leader welcomed the group to the Annual Hanukkah Game Day. The rules and procedures were explained.

    a. Each student is assigned to a team by a name tag. The student with the star on the name tag is the team captain. The captain will maintain order for the team and will be responsible for the team scorecard. The team must move as a group at all times.

    b. The objective is to play each game and to receive as many points as possible.

    c. There are five gaming stations. The team must listen to and follow the rules at each station. Cooperation and fair play are essential. Orderliness and self control are expected at all times.

    d. Each game is completed in fifteen minutes. A bell will ring, play will stop, the team captain will present her scorecard to the teacher. The teacher will record the team's score. The captain will take the scorecard to the main scorecard (point it out) where each team's score will be recorded for each game by the administrative assistant.

    e. While the captain is doing this the rest of the team will move to the next station (counter-clockwise).

9. Students may ask the leader questions and clarify anything that has been said.

10. Students are then called forward by team numbers. Four teams are sent to each station (see set-ups page 78.)

11. When the bell rings each teacher explains the rules of the game in her area and play begins.

12. At the end of fifteen minutes, the bell rings, play stops, scoring begins and the teams move to the next station.

13. When all of the teams have visited the five stations, the students are asked to sit in the middle of the gym floor.

14. The leader says a few words about the celebration of Hanukkah. One student from each class comes forward to light the class Hanukkah menorah which has been set out on a special table. The music teacher or another designated person leads the total group in singing the blessings. Two or three Hanukkah songs are sung. Meanwhile the administrative assistant, with the help of a calculator, is totaling the scores on the scoreboard.

15. The leader reads the list of top scores by team. Those teams line up at the refreshment table first. The students may then sit with anyone in the area to eat and play dreidel.

16. Ten minutes before dismissal all students clean up the area. The Game Day activity is scheduled for two hours.

NOTE: *We have participated in* <u>Hanukkah</u> *Game Day for many years. The students and the teachers rate the activity highly. The students enjoy the games and the social time. The teachers enjoy working as a group. Different Judaic content areas are covered. We have never had a discipline problem. The students are orderly and well behaved. The key is total staff involvement and training, very specific rules, and a tremendous amount of organization.*

HOLIDAY HORSERACES

OBJECTIVE:
Team will work together to gain the most points and to review facts about major holidays.

PROCEDURE:
1. Students sit together as teams.
2. The captain chooses one member to be the "horse" and to wear the team emblem and color.
3. The teacher spins the spinner. (Large circle is cut from posterboard. Circle is divided into 8 equal sections—each section is color-coded using 4 alternating colors). The team whose color the spinner indicates will answer the question.
4. The whole team can discuss the answer. The first answer given counts.
5. If the answer is correct, the horse moves ahead one furlong (furlongs consist of masking tape taped to the floor at two-foot intervals in a straight line). If the answer is incorrect, the horse does not move ahead. The teacher spins again and a new question is asked. The previous question may be used at a later time.
6. When the game ends, the team receives ten points for each furlong, with the first team crossing the finishing line receiving twenty-five extra points.

MATERIALS NEEDED:
Ten pieces of masking tape (eighteen inches each) placed on the floor two feet apart.
Four color-coded team emblems (cardboard dreidel with string to hang around "horse's" neck).
One large four-color-coded spinner (round shape cut from poster board with spinner—see instructions above).

ASKED AS QUESTIONS:

1. The name of King Ahasuerus' first wife? *Vashti*

2. The fall holiday on which we fast? *Yom Kippur*

3. The holiday on which we plant trees? *Tu b'Shevat*

4. The holiday remembering the Exodus? *Passover*

5. The holiday on which we eat in a booth? *Sukkot*

6. The holiday on which we march with the Torah? *Simhat Torah*

7. The holiday on which the Temple was rededicated? *Hanukkah*

8. The new year holiday? *Rosh HaShanah*

9. The special cookie eaten on Purim? *Hamantashen*

10. The fried pancake eaten on Hanukkah? *Latkes*

11. The item we wave in all directions to show that God is everywhere? *Lulav*

12. The color associated with Yom Kippur? *White*

13. The queen who asked, "Why do you want to kill me?" *Esther*

14. The holiday that is the Day of Atonement? *Yom Kippur*

15. Thanksgiving is based on this holiday? *Sukkot*

16. The bad guy in the Hanukkah story? *Antiochus*

17. The holiday on which we received the Ten Commandments? *Shavuot*

18. The holiday on which we use the Haggadah? *Passover*

19. Queen Esther's cousin? *Mordechai*

20. Special braided bread eaten on Shabbat? *Hallah*

21. Prophet who visits on Passover? *Elijah*

22. Holiday on which we eat apples and honey? *Rosh HaShanah*

23. *"Borei p'ri hagafen"* ends which prayer? *Kiddush*

24. The service at which we use the spice box? *Havdalah*

25. Holiday on which we light 44 candles? *Hanukkah*

26. Holiday celebrating Israel's Independence? *Yom Ha-Atzmaut*

27. Event observed on *Yom Ha-Shoah? Holocaust*

28. Holiday called the Festival of Lots? *Purim*

CONCENTRATION

OBJECTIVE:

To match the most cards, earning 5 points for each match.

PROCEDURE:

1. Team sits together and numbers members one to five. Each player will match cards *without* input from other team members.

2. Using a chart rack and pocket chart, 3"x5" cards are numbered and placed in the chart as illustrated on page 70. Behind each numbered card another will be placed with one of the statements listed. They will be placed in random order.

NOTE: A rebus (picture puzzle) may also be used. These pictures are placed in order beneath the statement cards. Blank cards are inserted between the pictures so that every statement card has a picture or blank card behind it.

ANOTHER NOTE: Younger students can play concentration with matching picture cards instead of statement cards, eliminating the rebus.

3. The teacher asks team one, player number one, to choose two numbers. If the concepts match, the student is given the two cards to hold. Rebus pictures or blanks are revealed. The total team may then try to guess the rebus. When the rebus is solved, that team receives 25 extra points. Meanwhile, if a match was made, team one, player number two, may then choose two numbers. Repeat the same procedure through the sequence of team one's players as long as they continue to choose cards that match.

4. If the match is not correct, then player number one from team two may choose a pair of cards. If the match is correct, follow the above procedure. If it is not and the number one players have played, the number two players from each team play.

5. When all of the cards are matched and the rebus is solved, the students add up their matches. They receive 5 points for each correct match.

CONCEPTS

1. Greek Culture and Way of Life.............Hellenism
2. Ruler of Syria.......................................Antiochus
3. A Great Miracle Happened There.........Dreidel
4. Scene of Maccabean Revolt................Modin
5. Hanukkah Song...................................Rock of Ages
6. 8 Candles and 1 Shamash..................Menorah
7. Hammer...Judah Maccabee
8. Gift..Gelt
9. Tzedakah ....Keren Ami
10. Festival of Lights ....Hanukkah

MATERIALS NEEDED:

chart holder
pocket chart
3"x5" cards—
top layer   = numbers
middle layer = concepts
bottom layer = rebus
           spread
           throughout
           and blank
           cards inter-
           spersed

1	2	3	4	5
6	7	8	9	10
11	12	13	14	15
16	17	18	19	20

REBUS

CELEBRATE HANUKKAH WITH GIFTS FOR THE POOR CHILDREN.

67

SPIN THE DREIDEL—LAS VEGAS STYLE

Sam Hollander

OBJECTIVE:

To play dreidel and earn points.

PROCEDURE:

1. Students sit on the floor with their team members.

2. The teacher tells everyone to spin his or her dreidel.

3. When all of the dreidels stop spinning, the teacher spins her dreidel. She announces which side is up.

4. Everyone whose dreidel has landed with the same side up as the teacher's receives a marker.

5. When the time for playing has expired, the teacher counts each student's markers and records five points for each marker.

MATERIALS NEEDED:

One dreidel for each child and teacher.

Markers (poker chips, play money, etc.)

JEOPARDY

OBJECTIVE:

To state questions to the given answers.

To review curricular material.

PROCEDURE:

1. Students sit as a team. Each team numbers its players one to five.
2. Four chairs are set up in front of a game board. A toy musical instrument is placed on each chair.
3. To begin, the number one players from each team sit in the front chairs.
4. One of these players is asked to pick a category.
5. The teacher removes the lowest point card in this category to reveal an answer. (Student says, "I want Bible for ten points") Within a category the point value of the cards progresses from the lowest to the highest. Students may move to different categories.
6. Any one of the four players may give the correct response.
    A. First she must make a noise with the musical instrument.
    B. The teacher recognizes the player whose instrument she hears first.
    C. The player must give her response in the form of a question. For example: If the card reads "Five Books of Moses", an appropriate answer may be, "What is in the Torah?" or "What are Genesis, Exodus, Leviticus, Numbers and Deuteronomy called?"
7. If the response is correct, that team receives the points indicated. Then the number two players from each team replace the number ones. The team receiving the points for the first card may now pick the new category.
8. If the response is incorrect, the points indicated are subtracted from the team's points. Other players may then answer. If no one among the players knows the correct answer, then anyone from the total group may answer, but points are not given. If no one knows the correct answer, the teacher should state it. Then the next set of players come forward and a new category is chosen.

MATERIALS NEEDED:

Four Toy Musical Instruments (drum, maracas, triangle, cymbal, etc.)

Chart rack and pocket chart

Numbers and answer cards

BIBLE	ISRAEL	PATRIARCHS	MOSES	KINGS
10	10	10	10	10
20	20	20	20	20
30	30	30	30	30
40	40	40	40	40
50	50	50	50	50

JEOPARDY QUESTIONS

CATEGORY	SUGGESTED ANSWERS	QUESTIONS
BIBLE	10—5 Books of Moses	What is the Torah?
	20—Leviticus	What is the third book in the Bible?
	30—Hebrew	In what language is the Bible written?
	40—39	How many books are in the Bible?
	50—Torah, Prophets, Writings	What is Tanakh?
ISRAEL	10—1948	In what year did Israel become a state?
	20—David ben Gurion	Who was the first Prime Minister?
	30—Jews, Christians, Moslems	Which three religious groups call Jerusalem their holy city?
	40—Leading seaport	What is Haifa?
	50—Camp David Peace Accord	What was the meeting for peace with Egypt called?
PATRIARCHS	10—Was kind to strangers	Who was Abraham?
	20—Abraham's two sons	Who were Isaac and Ishmael?
	30—God doesn't want human sacrifices	What does the story of Isaac's sacrifice teach?
	40—Twin sons of Isaac	Who were Jacob and Esau?
	50—"Mess of pottage"	For what did Esau sell his birthright?
MOSES	10—Mt. Sinai	Where did Moses receive the Ten Commandments?
	20—Heard the voice of God	What happened at the Burning Bush?
	30—Holiday connected with Exodus	What is Passover?
	40—Aaron	Who spoke to Pharaoh for Moses?
	50—Death of firstborn son	Which plague convinced Pharaoh to let the Hebrews go?
KINGS	10—First king of Israel	Who was Saul?
	20—Built the Temple	What did Solomon do?
	30—Made Jerusalem the Capital	What did David do?
	40—After Solomon	When did the kingdom split?
	50—Prophet who told David he was not above the Law	Who was Nathan?

MATCH GAME

OBJECTIVE:

To match the answers of the leader and to earn the most points.

PROCEDURE:

1. Teams sit together. The team numbers its players one to five. All players have ten 3"x5" cards and a dark colored marker.
2. Four chairs are placed in front of the group so that the people sitting in them will have their backs to their team.
3. The number one players from each team will sit in the chairs.
4. The teacher will state a category, for example: "Name a city in Israel."
5. The students on each team will respond by writing the word that they think their number one player will write. After they write their answers they will raise their hands so that the teacher knows who has finished.
6. When all hands are up, the teacher asks members of one team to read what they wrote and to hold up their cards. Then she asks the number one player to read her card. If her answer matches with one team player they receive five points, with two players—ten points, with three players—fifteen points and if they all agree—twenty-five points. She does the same with all teams. The teacher keeps a tally of the teams' points.
7. The number two players take the front seats and play continues.

MATERIALS NEEDED:

3"x5" cards (at least ten for each student—both sides may be used), one dark colored marker for each student.

LIST OF CATEGORIES:

a city in Israel	something you would like to see in Israel
a famous person in Israel's history	a famous building or landmark in Israel
a Jewish food	something found in the synagogue
something Jewish in your home	a Jewish book
a Jewish song	a man found in the Bible
a woman found in the Bible	a Federation agency
a Jewish holiday	a Jewish scientist
a Jewish entertainer	something associated with Passover

GAME DAY SET-UP
MASTER SET-UP

serving tables

XXXXX   XXXXX
XXXXX   XXXXX
||||||||||||
Holiday Horserace

Spin the dreidel

Y

Match Game

XXXXX
XXXXX
XXXX
XXXXX
XXXXX

chart rack

XXXX
XXXX
XXXX
XXXX
Jeopardy

Concentration

chart rack

XXXX
XXXX

XXXX
XXXX

x = chair   Y = table for <u>H</u>anukkah Menorah.   Colorful game sign at each station

TEAM SCORECARD

HOLIDAY HORSERACE	
SPIN THE DREIDEL	
CONCENTRATION	
JEOPARDY	
MATCH GAME	
TOTAL	

Laminated for reuse. Each teacher has an eraseable marker.

MAIN SCORECARD

TEAMS	HORSERACE	DREIDEL	CONCENTRATION	JEOPARDY	MATCH	TOTAL
1						
2						
3						

Materials needed laminated for reuse, erasable markers, calculator

11.
EFFECTIVE FIELD TRIPS

ield trips must be planned with the same attention to details and the overall picture as any lesson. The planner should ask the following questions:

1. Why do I want the children to experience this trip?
2. Can they get this information in another way?
3. What are the specific goals for the trip?
4. What are the best ways to achieve these goals?

After these questions are answered, and only then, the planner is ready to begin gathering information, preparing students and staff, and arranging all the practical details of implementation.

EXAMPLE: *The Precious Legacy*, a wonderful museum exhibit, was coming to the Miami area. Jewish artifacts from Czechoslovakia would be on display for a few weeks. We knew that every Jewish school and organization that could would be scheduling trips to the museum. The Bass Museum is located in South Beach where many of our Jewish elderly and Holocaust survivors reside. We knew that they would be anxious to visit the museum also. We began our planning.

As the principal, I decided that I would like to offer this experience to our seventh and eighth graders, because they would be mature enough to handle the experience and because they had all been exposed to an excellent ten week mini-course on the Holocaust.

73

I polled the seventh and eighth grade teachers to see if their teaching schedules could be altered to fit in the trip. I needed their support for this venture. They had all read the write-up about the exhibit in the newspaper and they were excited to be a part of the excursion.

I phoned the museum to reserve a date toward the end of the showing. I found out that I could bring 120 students, that the exhibit would be displayed on two floors, and that the museum would not provide docents. This was important information. This meant that the students would walk through the exhibit, read the placards if they chose to do so, and they would be herded along with the regular patrons of the museum.

I made plans with the teachers to meet for lunch after Religious School the first weekend that the exhibit opened. The school supplied box lunches. We drove to Miami Beach in two cars. We noted the time that it took and the area where we could park the buses. This is important information for the planning process.

The teachers' assignment was to enjoy the exhibit, study it closely and to make suggestions in writing as to how we could best present it to the students. It was important that the teachers use this time to view the exhibit leisurely. When escorting 120 students the teachers would not have the opportunity to enjoy the exhibit. That would be working time. We rented the hand-held speaker wands that serve as guides as you move through the museum. We agreed that this was not an efficient or interesting way to learn about the exhibit. We would not use them for the students. We noted the sections in which the artifacts were displayed, the time needed to view them, things that we found to be exceptionally interesting to us, and those that we thought the students might really like.

The teachers submitted their suggestions and we discussed the possibilities for success and failure. By this time the teachers had bought into the project. They were a part of the planning and decision making process.

During the week I called the museum and spoke to the director. It was time to work with the person with the most authority. I explained to her who we were and what we were trying to achieve. The staff and I did not feel that walking through and viewing the displays would meet our educational needs. I told her what we wanted to do. She said that no other group had done what we wanted to do and that it might be difficult. I promised her that our plan would work, that the students would be well behaved, and that the teachers would be totally prepared. It would be a wonderful educational experience, but we needed her help. She asked me to put the plan in writing and she would consider it. I did as she asked and benefitted from her expertise and concessions.

The museum provided us with background material, teacher's guides and slides of many artifacts. We received a copy of the script that we heard on the speaker wands.

There were seven sections to the exhibit. The teachers would become docents. They were given the opportunity to choose an area or to be assigned one. They received a copy of the master plan, a map of the exhibit, and their section of the script. They were told to read their scripts carefully and to choose only that information that they thought would be most interesting to the students or that could be best illustrated by the displayed artifacts. The whole script would be too long and too boring for the students. The students would be in their section for approximately six minutes.

Publicity letters and flyers were sent home one month before the target date. The students were told about the trip in class.

Seven parent chaperones would be needed. The volunteers received a detailed letter listing their responsibilities, the master plan and a map of the museum. When parents know exactly what is expected of them they can be real helpers instead of tag-alongs. They appreciate being a part of the process also.

Buses were ordered. Exact locations, pick-up and delivery times were stated. Permission slips and money were collected.

The week before the trip one teacher assumed the responsibility for a special assembly. He presented historical background information, slides illustrating what we would see, and the plan for implementing the trip so that the students would know what would happen and what would be expected of them.

During the week the list of students was used to prepare color coded name tags for each student, parents, and teacher. Using seven different colored markers one teacher, one parent, and seventeen students were assigned to each group. Three staff people were not assigned groups as they would be stationed at strategic places throughout the museum to handle any problems that might arise.

On the day of the trip everyone put on their name tag upon arrival at school. They knew who were in their group and that the groups could not be changed. Potential discipline problems were averted. Each teacher and parent had a list of students in their group.

At the appropriate time the students boarded the buses. At this time they could sit with whomever they chose regardless of color tag. Bus rules which were stated at the assembly were reviewed on each bus.

  a. No radios were permitted on the bus.
  b. Hands and arms must remain in the bus.
  c. Tushes must remain in the seat.
  d. No loud voices were permitted.

Arrangements were made in advance so that the museum would be open to our group one half hour before the regular patrons would be admitted. This was a wonderful concession for us as we knew that once the regular visitors arrived it would be more difficult to control our 120 students. One check for all fees was presented to the museum.

The total group watched a 25-minute videotape which provided the information needed to appreciate the exhibit. Upon completion each color group was called forward and sent to one of the seven areas of the museum with the teacher and parent. This was a super concession to us on the part of the museum as all their groups began at point A and followed the route to the end. We were able to avoid having 120 students in the same area waiting for the line in front of them to move. We would also avoid the problem of part of the group finishing before the others.

Each teacher now spoke about his or her section of the museum like an expert. They could point out interesting details, ask questions of their students, and answer inquiries. Some of the teachers even did additional research work and had a wealth of interesting facts and inferences to share.

The unassigned staff members could roam the exhibit and take a reading as to how long was really necessary at each area. At the appropriate time, a little bell was rung and each group of students, with a parent, moved to the next display area. Each adult had a map of the museum and the path that they were to take. Each parent was prepared to keep the students moving in an orderly manner. The teachers remained at their areas, receiving a new group of students and repeating their presentations to all seven groups.

By this time the museum was open to the public. These new arrivals thought that our staff members were museum employees and at times they would interrupt with questions and comments. They were gently told that our teachers were not with the museum, but with the temple, and that the public could listen, but could not be a part of the group. The teachers received many compliments on how wonderful they were and were told that they should be hired by the museum. This made them feel great.

All seven groups finished at the same time and returned to the buses. We had no discipline problems or incidents throughout the morning. Interest was high and the students enjoyed seeing the artifacts that they had seen on the slides the week before. Students, parents, and teachers rated the experience as excellent.

Crowd control is important, but it must be planned well in advance with each person knowing exactly what is expected of him/her at all times. Problems can arise, but if the basics are under control, then the person in charge only has to worry about "the problem," not about a situation where everything is falling apart.

During the next session of school, the teachers reviewed the experience with the students. They discussed the highlights of the exhibit. Students shared their favorite artifacts and why they enjoyed them.

To review, for a successful field trip:

1. Visit the place in advance. Call first and know who your contact person will be. Go to the place and meet with the person if necessary. Discuss your objectives, special needs and problems.

2. Know the basics:

    a. How long will the trip take?

    b. Where will you park the cars or buses? How many will you need?

    c. Which door will the group enter?

    d. Which on-site person will meet the group?

    e. What will the group see or do?

    f. How long will the activity take?

    g. How many support personnel will be needed?

    h. What problems may arise?

    i. What preparation is needed for the students, teachers, parents?

    j. What publicity, permission slips, money or information will be needed?

    k. What is the master plan for the experience?

    l. What follow-up activities are needed?

    m. Remember to send thank you notes to all adults involved including those at the place visited.

12.
USING GUEST SPEAKERS

Guest speakers are a wonderful addition to the school curriculum. These are people with firsthand knowledge of a situation because they have lived through it or they are experts in a particular area. They are new faces to the students and speak with authority on their subjects.

Speakers can be secured from the temple membership list, a questionnaire to parents asking about their experiences and skills, local agencies, write-ups on local people in the newspaper or referrals. Do not overlook recommendations from the teaching staff or using the staff as speakers in classrooms other than their own.

Sometimes it is possible to secure a person who lived during an historical moment. The sharing of personal experiences will give the students greater insight into this period and will help make it come alive for them. For example, a holocaust survivor, a Jewish immigrant from Cuba, a former cult member, or a civil rights activist will each illuminate the events they experienced for your students.

Guest speakers are chosen because they are experts in a particular field. For example, the rabbi speaks on Torah, God, prayer, rabbinical training. A member of a kibbutz or a person who worked with Ethiopian Jews could share slides and experiences. Temple board members, Federation members and heads of Jewish communal service organizations can tell about their jobs or volunteer positions and why they were attracted to them. These people are excellent role models for our students.

Guest speakers should be contacted in person or by telephone. The date, time, subject, objectives and questions to be addressed should be discussed. The speaker should know how many students will be present, the age of the group, course of study, and time frame needed. It should be decided whether the speaker will answer questions and whether this should occur during or after the presentation. Information to use in an introduction should be secured. Requests for equipment or special set-up should be noted. Inquire if an honorarium is expected so that you can plan accordingly. All of this should be followed by a letter to the speaker confirming the above.

Example of information given to an immigrant who is to visit a class:

Students in a Jewish Roots in America class have been studying Jewish immigration to America. They have read and discussed the problems of immigration and the decisions that families must make when they either choose or are forced to leave their place of birth. The object of your presentation is to personalize the immigration experience. Please use the following questions as a guide.

1. Describe the Jewish community in your native country.

2. Why did you leave your country and choose to come to America?

3. Describe the problems that you encountered in leaving your country and how you overcame them.

4. What problems, adjustments, and adventures did you have when settling in America?

5. How did you become involved in the Jewish community in America?

Please bring in pictures or foods or artifacts from your native country that you can share with the students.

Example of information given to the rabbi who visited a class:

Inter-office note to the rabbi who will be leading the fifth grade classes on a tour of the Western Wall.

During our Touring Israel curriculum section on Jerusalem, we will be visiting the Wall. The students will have seen a slide presentation on Jerusalem and will have been exposed to Jerusalem as a city holy to three major religions. Please meet the class at the wall by the playground. REMEMBER, WE ARE IN JERUSALEM! The teachers will bring *kippot* for the boys and will separate the boys from the girls as we approach the Wall. During your presentation, welcome them to Jerusalem and the Wall, describe security measures, the history of the Wall, its importance to our people in the past and to us today. Describe what they are seeing: the height of the Wall, the people, a bar mitzvah, prayer groups, etc. Reserve time for prayer and note writing. Let's discuss.

Example of information given to the Temple Board Member who is to visit a class:

Students in a Comparative Judaism class learn that all branches of Judaism have a professional staff. However, they must also have lay leadership and volunteers if they are to be successful. These people are needed to form policy, raise funds, and work on committees. Please join us for brunch on (date). You will be teamed with four students. Please discuss leadership, motivation for service and the need to help one's temple. Use the following questions as a guide.

1. What is the purpose of the Temple Board?
2. How are board members chosen?
3. What is your position on the board?
4. What are you required to do?
5. What other things have you done for the temple?
6. Why have you chosen to become involved in the temple?
7. What has this involvement done for you?
8. Why should the students become involved in the temple?

Guest speakers should be evaluated and files should be kept so that they can be invited to return in the future. Thank you notes should be sent along with students' comments or "Dear Speaker" letters. Donations to the speaker's organization or to the temple can be made if an honorarium was not requested.

DEAR MRS. HERMAN, DEAR RABBI, DEAR GUEST SPEAKER:

There are many times that we bring guest speakers into the classroom to lead a discussion or share information with the students. It is important that the session is not just a lecture, but an interaction. We have invited Jews from other countries to discuss their immigration experiences with our students studying Jewish Roots in America. They have brought in books, pictures and artifacts from their native countries in addition to their stories. Holocaust survivors share their awesome tale of moving from concentration camps to freedom. Jews by choice describe their journey into a new religion. Members of the Catholic Church share their upbringing and beliefs as Catholics. Before we hired our first woman rabbi, we invited our county's first woman rabbi to tell about her experiences and her motivation for entering the rabbinate. We also invite our staff rabbis into the classroom on a regular basis.

We follow up many of these sessions with a "Dear _____" letter. These letters are a summary of what the student learned from the experience. The students are told that this is a way of evaluating the session. We need to know if they learned what we had intended. The letters are read by the teacher and the principal and are evaluated. We then decide if the speaker and the subject have been of interest to the students and if it should be repeated with other groups in the future. The letters are then sent to the speaker so that she can have feedback. This model can be used with all guest speakers.

The following are two examples of how we used this activity.

One of our seventh-grade classes studies Comparative Judaism. Many of our students have attended our schools since preschool and some have attended our day school before entering the Religious School track in junior high. They have been in our sanctuary numerous times. During this unit I tell the students and their parents about the history of the temple and then I take them on a tour of the campus and the sanctuary. The objectives are to show them the uniqueness of our sanctuary, to compare the customs of a Reform temple and those of our friends who attend Conservative or Orthodox synagogues, to examine the ritual objects and to retell the stories and legends associated with our history. My hope is that the students and parents will come away feeling that the sanctuary is theirs, that it is a special place where one behaves differently than in other places, and that they have new knowledge that they can share with their family and friends.

Below are excerpts from the students "Dear Mrs. Herman" letters written after my visit.

"This morning I really learned a lot. I had never been up in the choir loft and I really enjoyed it . The plaques that I saw were very interesting and how people cared enough to donate money for it. I had never known about the bullet holes and now I do. The menorah with spears was very clever and original."

"I learned a lot from your tour and discussion. I learned about the memorial plaque and how the names light up on the anniversary of the person's death. The sequences of the stained glass windows, the history of the menorah and the story about the seven bullet holes intrigued me. I now know many things about the synagogue that I didn't know before. The needlepoint picture about King David was beautiful as well as the artwork that was on display. The story about the eternal light and how Rabbi Baumgard found it was interesting. Thank you for spending your time to take us on a memorable tour."

"I learned a lot about the synagogue. The tour was interesting. I didn't know about the stained glass window where the morning light comes through..."

"...I always thought that the letters on the ark were just letters. I didn't really know that they meant anything. I also think it's fascinating that the menorot and the ark and the ner tamid are the only ones like them in the world. I also never knew that half the things in this temple were donated. I thought that you and the other staff just went out and bought everything."

"...I learned about Mark Light and how they put up a building for him. And I have been a member here for almost all of my life and I never learned most of the things that you taught us today and things like that, which we will remember as long as we are at this temple and that's what makes me proud to be here at Temple Beth Am."

Another seventh-grade class has Breakfast With the Rabbi to discuss "Where was God during the Holocaust?" Below are some of the responses found in the "Dear Rabbi" letters.

"Today I learned what God really meant. The rabbi taught us about the holocaust and God, and how they are both related. This discussion in depth brought out my feeling of God and what I do and don't believe about Him in my mind. Now I will probably think about God in many more and different ways."

"...Do we pray to God for material things? Well, if we think He is a magician and always makes everything good, then we would be disappointed that He wasn't there to help us in a time of struggle. He does not have the power to make the order of the universe change no matter how much someone prays. He only has the power to unleash the good in all of us."

"...I learned that God is not here to ask Him to pass an exam or to make it sunny. The time God is here for you is when you really need Him like if someone is sick in your family and not for selfish praying. But, He is not always going to be able to help."

"...I was surprised to see that everyone including myself was quiet. There were things that I wanted to say that I didn't because I was shy and embarrassed and I know that there is nothing to be embarrassed about."

"...I learned about the real purpose and meaning of prayer. I also learned that God will not change the natural order of things because of a prayer, and that through education and wisdom people can make the choice between good and evil."

These letters and the others that the students write help the speakers see how the students perceive them, understand what they are teaching, feel about themselves and the concepts covered. This is valuable information that can be used for evaluating lessons and for planning future curricula.

13.
USING ROLE PLAY AND
SOCIO-DRAMA

ocio-drama provides an excellent vehicle for student involvement. During a socio-drama the students assume the roles of other persons. They are asked to put aside their own identities, feelings and thoughts and to literally become the "others." They are put into a structured environment, where time, place, and events are described. As they become these other persons they are asked to act and react as the "others" would and not as they would if they were themselves. This activity can deal with social problems, interpersonal conflicts, historical events or any situation where the class would benefit from role playing. This activity encourages maximum participation, a higher level of thinking, and creativity. Many times students will not become involved in a discussion or situation if they play themselves as they do not want to risk sharing their own feelings. Socio-drama lets them become involved as someone else.

The following socio-drama was designed to involve the students in a particular period of history—the end of the Golden Age of Spain.

In the textbook, *The History of the Jews in America*, by Deborah Pessin, United Synagogue of America, we read:

...It happened in Spain, in the summer of 1492. All day they kept coming down to the sea, some in orderly procession, some in confused groups huddled together. All day they streamed out of the provinces of Spain onto the open highways...On March 30 of that year King Ferdinand and Queen Isabella had issued the Edict of Expulsion, giving the Jews four months to dispose of their possessions and leave Spain...Leave all that they had built during the hundreds of years they had lived in Spain. Leave their homes...meadows...synagogues...academies...cemeteries...."

What would this mean to the seventh-graders who were learning about this important period of Jewish history? What do they know about having to leave their country? What do they know about selling homes and property, giving up professions and jobs, leaving relatives and friends behind as they carry everything they can to a place unknown? How do you capture a moment in history that would become a turning point for the Jewish people?

This is where a socio-drama can be very useful. The teacher chooses that moment and creates a situation that will put the students in that place with the problems that the people had to face.

The teacher must be very specific in what he wants to achieve through this activity. He must list the objectives that are to be accomplished.

EDICT OF EXPULSION

OBJECTIVES:

The students will:

1. Experience decision making involving leaving one's home under duress.
2. List the opportunities available to them.
3. List their choices of action.
4. Share their feelings of "being there."

The teacher then decides how he will meet these objectives. His role is to set up the situation, assign roles, give directions, provide materials and state what is expected of the group. He then removes himself from active participation while the students become totally involved. Keeping all of this in mind, read the following to see how it works.

PREPARATION:

The teacher creates roles for each student in the class. For this socio-drama the following information is included: the name of the person, his or her place in a family, age, job, economic status, religion and health (see page 97). There will be a name tag which will identify the person and his religion. Props or materials that will enhance the socio-drama will also need to be prepared (newspaper, see page 95).

The teacher also establishes an environment for the socio-drama. For this socio-drama a large classroom may be used. Movable desks will be needed as they will be arranged according to family groups. The teacher will need a chalkboard to list the tasks and to debrief at the end of the activity.

PROCEDURE:

1. The students are assigned seats. (The room has been set up in family groups. An envelope containing information on the student's role is on each desk.) The students are told that for this exercise they will each have the opportunity to become a new person. Their names, family members, and details of their lives will be in the envelopes on their desks. They open the envelopes, put on their name tags and read about themselves and their families. Some of the family members will not be represented by actual students, but they will be taken into consideration when decisions are made. Students representing Jews will wear yellow star name tags. Non-Jews will wear a brown triangle name tag. The students are instructed to become that person for the rest of class. All of their reactions, interactions and decisions are to be based on their being this new person.

2. The teacher then sets up the situation. She gives a short description of the political climate in the United States, a few years in the future. She tells the class that the United States has recently been involved in a major confrontation with China. Nuclear weapons were not used. However, this confrontation has been costly in terms of money, men, and prestige. Neither country won any significant gains. During these years, the President of the United States has gradually exercised more and more power which has not been approved by Congress. This is a very popular president and the citizens trusted the President's decisions. There has been little opposition to his new and absolute power. It is now time for the country to heal its wounds and to come together to rebuild the sagging spirit of the country. The media reports that the President and Congress will meet all night to chart a new course for the United States.

It is early morning. Your newspaper has been delivered. Remember, you are now the person described in the envelope. Your assignment is to read the morning newspaper (page 95) and do the following:

NOTE: *These are listed on the board and are read aloud by the teacher.*

1. Do not talk to family members. Write your reactions and your feelings on paper. (Paper and pencils will be on a desk in the family group.)

2. Then discuss the events with your family members, if you have a family.
3. List the opportunities available to you and your family.
4. List what you will do and why you chose to do this.

The teacher should ask if there are any questions. The teacher answers these and then removes herself from the action. The students will need approximately twenty minutes to complete their assignment. The teacher can quietly listen in on the discussion and make notes on interesting interactions in the groups.

An important step in socio-drama is to pull it all together. Students should have the opportunity to respond. It is the teacher's role to keep them on task and not to permit discussion to ramble. Using a chalkboard to summarize major points can be very helpful.

At the end of the time allowed, the teacher will role-play a reporter for "World Wide News." She will conduct interviews with members of the community as to their reactions and decisions. She will list their responses on the chalkboard under the headings: FEELINGS AND REACTIONS, OPPORTUNITIES, FINAL DECISION. Each area is discussed.

Props, such as a tape recorder, videocamera or even a pretend microphone can add to the atmosphere of the activity. The students will enjoy seeing or hearing themselves when the socio-drama is completed.

One of the purposes of a socio-drama is to give the students the opportunity to live another "life" and react to it. Having "been there" they should be able to be active participants in follow-up discussion and their contributions should be on a higher level than if they just read about the event.

The following areas were chosen for discussion:

...Could a situation like this really occur? (Use as a lead into the end of the Golden Age of Spain and the Edict of Expulsion. Adapt to the Holocaust or any other time when Jews were forced to leave their homes. Comment on the Japanese internment during World War II.)

...What criteria or values did you consider when making your decision? (money, land, religion, health, children, employment)

...Did you consider helping other Jewish families in your community? Did you make an effort to come together as a group? Did you try to help others less fortunate than yourself? Are there Jewish organizations that can help us in troubled times?

...What will happen to your homes, property, offices and other things that you cannot take with you? How much will these things be worth if everyone's possessions go on the market at the same time? What would you take with you?

88

THE MIAMI HERALD

Tuesday, March 15, 19__   Florida's Complete Newspaper

NON-CHRISTIANS MUST LEAVE U.S.A.

President Benson called a Special Meeting of Congress last night. In a surprise speech the President stated a new and forceful dictate, "Due to our recent war with China and knowing that we will probably be faced with a similar situation again, it has become necessary to do everything we can to unify our nation. Therefore, we will become 'one nation under God!' Other nations will witness us as we join forces, bind our wounds, and unite to rebuild our spirit. This next month will be important as we show the world that through our faith we can overcome any adversity that faces us. This next month will be a time for all of us to put America first...a time to truly melt into one.

Those of us in responsible governmental positions and in the armed forces will do all that we can to help our fellow countrymen put Christian America first. A nation that prays together stays together. Those who do not wish to become true believers will have one month from today to leave our shores. We must make every effort to con-

PRESIDENT BENSON'S COMPLETE MESSAGE

on Page 2

vert those who wish to remain." The President ended his historic speech with a call for all citizens to be "one." The

President will appear on national television tonight at 7:30 P.M. on all channels and on all radio stations to outline procedures for our spiritual revival, for government conversion centers, and for those wishing to leave the United States. Congress gave the President a standing ovation.

JEWISH CONGRESSMEN SHAKEN

Senators Cohen and Landau and Representative Rabin joined each other at the close of the meeting of the Congress. Senator Cohen is quoted as saying, "I can't believe that this is happening. We have given the President more and more power as the war deepened. This power was to preserve our freedom, not take it away. We have made a grave mistake. Now our congressmen have turned into a bunch of yes-men." Representative Rabin shook her head sadly, "We, the Jewish people, have contributed so much to this country. Our constitution is all but dead."

ORIENTALS TOLD PLAN

All citizens of Asian ancestry were told of President Benson's newest dictate in the San Francisco Center where they have been since the outbreak of the war with China. Many of these people are descendants of settlers of the 1800's and they are still con-

fused as to why their loyalty to the U.S. was questioned when we went to war with China. Again their loyalty is being questioned. This time they can prove their loyalty, if those who are not already Christians become believers.

...Where can you go to begin a new life? What problems would you encounter? (new culture, little money and possessions, strange language, resentment of residents)

...Do the Jews need a homeland? (role of Israel, Law of Return)

...Now that you have encountered this situation, what have you learned about the need for personal commitment to our Constitution? For taking an active role in the government process? For awareness, to become thinking, knowledgeable citizens? For taking care of the Jewish community?

This socio-drama and others like it totally involve the students in the learning process. They are put in situations where they must think and decide their fate. Everyone has something to do. Now they are ready to read about this period in history. They can feel for those people in 1492 who streamed out of the provinces of Spain, leaving their world behind them as they struggled with a new life in the new world.

The people, property, and situations in our socio-drama reflect life in South Florida. Since the students will become the people described on the cards, it is important that the student's are given information that they can relate to. The specifics can be changed to fit any community.

THE CHARACTERS:

SARAH LEVINE, Age 65
JACOB LEVINE, Age 68

You live in a condominium on Miami Beach. Jacob is a retired restaurant owner from the Catskill Mountains in New York. Sarah worked with Jacob to make it a highly successful business. You have enough money to live comfortably and to travel up north to visit your children and grandchildren. You have been to Israel and Europe. Sarah has considerable jewelry which is kept in the bank vault. You have a fairly active social life in the condo—cards, parties, Jewish organizations. You have no major investments, just some small stocks. You have $20,000 in your savings and checking account. Sarah is in good health. Jacob recently had bypass heart surgery.

ROSE RICHMAN, Age 82

You are a widow and live alone in a one-room efficiency on Miami Beach. You have no immediate family in Florida. You live on Social Security and food stamps. You go to the free lunch program sponsored by the Jewish Vocational Service Meals Program. You own few clothes and possessions. You have a wedding ring and an engagement ring. You spend most of your day walking on Washington Avenue looking for bargains and you go to the Jewish Community Center for senior activities. At night you watch your 10-year-old black-and-white television. Your health is fair. You suffer from poor eyesight and arthritis.

ANDY SIMPSON, Age 20

You are a student at the University of Miami majoring in engineering. Your hometown is Silver Springs, Maryland. You belong to a Jewish fraternity and have many friends. Your parents send you money for expenses and you drive a nice car. You have some jewelry and bonds that you received for birthdays and at your bar mitzvah ceremony. You are a good student and are in excellent health.

KAREN BUSHOFF, Age 25

You are an intern at Jackson Memorial Hospital. You have a promising career as an eye surgeon. You live at the hospital. You went through school on loans and scholarships and hope to earn enough money to repay these and care for your widowed mother. You do not own anything of value except a used car. You earn $18,000 yearly.

SHARON MANDLER, Age 48
BERNIE MANDLER, Age 49

You own your home in a nice section of South Miami. Bernie works for a large accounting firm and earns $50,000 a year. Sharon works as a substitute teacher a few days a week. You always wanted to visit Israel and you have saved enough to do this over the summer. You have put three children through college and you helped your son-in-law start a business. You have $15,000 in the bank, some jewelry and good stocks. You are both in good health.

DENNIS SMITH, Age 22
GAYLE SMITH, Age 21

Dennis is a Baptist. Gayle is Jewish. You have been married for two and one half years and have chosen to raise your children as Jews. Dennis works in his father's manufacturing plant which will be his when his father retires in five years. Gayle does not work. You have a baby girl who is one year old. You live in a lovely apartment among other newly married couples. You have two cars, good health and an extremely promising financial future.

JAMES DEAMPLE, Age 44
MARION DEAMPLE, Age 42
BOBBY, Age 15

James owns a concrete firm. His annual income is $75,000. He is active in the United Fund and the Masons. Marion is a member of the Daughters of the American Revolution and the Coral Gables Women's Club. You both are active in the First Methodist Church of Miami. They have three children. Two children are married and live in California. Bobby is fifteen years old and lives at home. He is a football player and a member of the National Honor Society. Everyone is in good health.

MARCIA ROCKOWITZ, Age 27
NORMAN ROCKOWITZ, Age 28

You have just moved into your first home in a new suburban development. You are members of a new Conservative synagogue. You have three children, ages five, two-and-one-half, and eight months. Norman is an up-and-coming attorney. Marcia was an art major and paints in her spare time. You have little money, little jewelry and no investments. You look forward to a great financial future, new friends, and roots in your new area. Everyone is in good health except the baby who is highly allergic.

RAFAEL MARCON, Age 48
SARITA MARCON, Age 46
JOSEPH MARCON, Age 17
DEENA MARCON, Age 14

Rafael was a lawyer in Cuba until Castro took over the government. Fleeing persecution and bullets, Rafael brought his family to the United States where he worked for his uncle in real estate. After many years he became a vice president of the firm. He has been a million dollar seller for five years. You are big supporters of Federation and the Cuban American Synagogue. The children have become Americanized, speak Spanish and English and enjoy a country club lifestyle. Sarita is active in the Cuban-Jewish Society and has adapted to American life. She employs full-time help in the house and plans numerous family vacations. You have a sizeable bank account and vast real estate holdings, including part ownership in two shopping centers. Everyone is in good health.

SANDRA BROWN, Age 42
CHAD BROWN, Age 45
ROY BROWN, Age 17
BRENDA BROWN, Age 15
FRED BROWN, Age 13

Sandra is a non-practicing Catholic. Chad is non-practicing Jew. They have been married for nineteen years. He manages a large Key Biscayne hotel. Sandra has returned to college to earn a degree in nursing. Roy is a senior and is applying for a place in a good university. Brenda is active in the major clubs in high school and is a cheerleader. Fred is an average junior high student. They live in a suburban area of Miami. The family has Christmas dinner and a tree. They go to Chad's parents' home for Passover. The children have not had a Religious School education. The family is active in community life and have modest savings. All are in good health.

ELLEN COSTER, Age 36
MARVIN COSTER, Age 39
STACI COSTER, Age 14
STEVE AND LARRY COSTER, Age 12 1/2

Marvin is a prominent young senator in the State House of Representatives. He is very actively politically and socially. He is a partner in successful law firm. He owns property and horses in Ocala, large stock holdings, and three homes (Miami, Tallahassee, and a large condo in Aspen). Ellen's family came to America in 1849 and have been leaders in the Reform Movement. She is active politically and socially also. She belongs to Hadassah, Sisterhood at their temple, Federation and the United Way. She owns stock in AT&T and Standard Oil. The three children have everything they want and do well in school. The boys are looking forward to their bar mitzvah in a few months.

RABBI PAUL KRAMER, Age 58
RHODA KRAMER, Age 52
JONAH KRAMER, Age 20
JOSHUA KRAMER, Age 19
SARA KRAMER, Age 15

Paul is the Rabbi in a large congregation. He earns $90,000+ a year. Rhoda is studying for a Master's Degree in psychology. They own their own home and three cars. They have modest savings, Israeli and American bonds. Jonah is studying at the University of Florida and is home on spring break. Joshua is interested in cars, girls, and having fun. Sara wants to be an actress. Another daughter, Deborah, is married with a new baby and lives in Boston.

14.

USING TRUE AND FALSE WORKSHEETS

Another way to totally involve students in a lesson and to heighten their interest in the subject is to use a True and False worksheet. Requiring each student to complete the paper means that she must read the material, think about the contents, and make a decision. If the concepts presented are of high interest or controversial, the students will want to know if their responses are correct.

DIRECTIONS FOR USE:

There should be no pressure or grade involved. The teacher will not evaluate the answers. The students complete this paper to see what they know and what they need to know. The questions will be discussed in class. Though the students are not expected to know the answers at the beginning of class, they will be expected to know them by the end of class. During discussion, the students may take notes and change their answers. *This is not a test. It is a learning tool.*

NOTE: *This technique can be used with any subject. The worksheet that follows is part of the* Jewish Life After Confirmation *curriculum. (See* Jewish Life After Confirmation: A *Course Curriculum, chapter* 20.)

PLACE A "T" FOR "TRUE" IN FRONT OF EACH CORRECT STATEMENT AND AN "F" FOR "FALSE" IN FRONT OF EACH STATEMENT THAT IS INCORRECT.

____1. Zero Population Growth means that a couple should not have children.

____2. Judaism considers marriage a form of holiness.

____3. Abortion is not permitted for Orthodox Jews.

____4. According to Jewish law a child is considered to be living from the moment of conception.

____5. Celibacy—not having sexual relations—is considered a form of holiness according to Jewish law.

____6. Jewish law dictates that when a mother and an unborn child are in danger, the mother's life is more important.

____7. Judaism actively seeks converts.

____8. An Orthodox rabbi must perform a conversion if it is to be acceptable in Israel.

____9. An Orthodox conversion insists that circumcision or mikvah take place.

___10. Temple Beth Am holds weekly conversion classes.

___11. No rabbi will marry a Jew and non-Jew.

___12. It is not important to evaluate your attitude towards material possessions before you marry as "love conquers all."

___13. We learn our role as a man or a woman from our parent's example.

___14. There are many Jewish diseases that we should be aware of before we marry.

Each of the topics on the worksheet is a lesson unto itself. A student will read the statement aloud and tell her answer. Others in the class will agree or disagree and all will have their say. This is the time for the teacher to explain, fill in information, quote Jewish sources, distribute handouts. It is an easy and effective way to motivate and cover many concepts. Because the students bought into the lesson when they answered the statements, they are extremely attentive and interested in the correct answer.

15.
INVOLVING PARENTS IN THE EDUCATIONAL PROCESS

The Religious School cannot educate the child alone. We need help from the home. Family education and parent involvement in the educational process can benefit the child, the family and the school. Among these benefits are:

- Children and parents build Jewish memories together.
- Parents show interest in the religious as well as the secular development of their children.
- Parents and children have the opportunity to learn and grow together.
- Parents will become more knowledgeable.
- Parents will acquire skills so that they can bring Jewish customs and traditions into the home.
- Parents can share ideas, concepts and beliefs with their children.
- Parents can reinforce what their child is learning.

- Parents will appreciate the need for religious education and will encourage their children to continue through Confirmation.

- Parents will see how religious education has changed since their school days and will appreciate the changes.

- Parents will be more supportive of the school.

- Parents may seek further education in adult studies classes.

The administration and the individual teacher should create opportunities to involve parents. An excellent resource for ideas can be found in Janice P. Alper's *Learning Together*. At our school we have tried the following with success.

Parents participate in holiday celebrations. They serve as room parents helping the teacher and students by preparing food, leading games and sharing learning sessions.

Parents are invited to school for special grade level parent days. During these sessions the teacher displays children's work and projects and will have time alone with the parents to discuss curriculum and expectations. The children spend this time with an enrichment teacher (art, music, dance etc.) and then return to complete a typical morning so that their parents can see them in action. Sometimes parents experience dance and music sessions with their children.

Parents visit for grade level special events. Our fourth-graders studying life cycle participate in a naming ceremony where they receive their Hebrew names. Third-graders invite parents to their Tzofim Introduction when they become Israeli scouts as part of their Children of Israel curriculum.

Parents serve as chaperones and learn with their children on field trips (visits to the Holocaust Memorial, Catholic church, Anne Frank exhibit) and are part of the audience when their children perform in plays and special events. We have also used parents as guest speakers with topics including social action, immigration, music, art, Israel, comedy, and Yiddish.

I particularly enjoy the interaction between students and parents when dialogues are set up so that both groups talk to each other on a sensitive subject. Our seventh grade course, From Generation to Generation, affords us the opportunity to invite parents to view a film, *Grandma Didn't Wave Back*. This film depicts the problems and agony of choosing to place an elderly relative in nursing home. The group cries together and shares experiences and the feelings that come with this decision. Many of our parents are part of the "sandwich generation" who, in addition to caring for their own children, must become the caretakers for their parents. They share the effect of this sandwiching with their children, perhaps for the first time. The students share their feelings for their parents and grandparents and the effect the situation has on them.

It is a powerful morning which everyone involved feels is very worthwhile. (*Generation to Generation*, Dorothy C. Herman, CAJE, Miami, Florida)

An eighth grade Comparative Religion class invites parents to share the last session with them. The parents have an opportunity to take the final exam that their child completed the week before so that they can become aware of the depth of the subject matter. Then both groups meet to review the answers and discuss the concepts. This is usually followed by a slide or film presentation. The group becomes heavily involved in a discussion of the differences and similarities between Jews and other religious groups. Conversions, interfaith dating, and cults, in addition to some of the parents' experiences in interfaith marriages keep the discussions lively.

Fifth- and sixth-graders and their parents are involved in a five-week Shabbat unit that culminates in a Shabbat dinner that is cooked by the students. Parents are required to attend two workshops where they experience learning with their child. They share, sing, learn blessings, view videos and help the children cook. Everyone helps with the dinner: preparing food, setting tables, serving and clearing. (*The Joy of Shaabbat*, Dorothy C. Herman, CAJE, Miami, Florida)

There are many wonderful family education projects being developed throughout our country as more and more educators are realizing the value of involving parents in the learning process. Resources are available from the University of Judaism, Whizin Institute in Los Angeles, California which hosts a week-long family education course each summer. The Torah Aura catalogue is also an excellent place to become familiar with packaged family education materials.

16.
STUDENT EVALUATION

Students, their work and progress, need to be evaluated. Students need to know that they are learning something and teachers need to know that they are really teaching something and not just talking about a subject. Evaluation is built into the lesson in the behavioral objectives section. There are many ways to evaluate what the student has accomplished.

For example, the objectives for a particular session might be stated in any of the following ways, all of which can be objectively measured or evaluated. At the end of the session, the student will (through writing)

    a.   be able to answer 80% of the questions correctly on the unit test.
    b.   be able to correctly complete the outline.
    c.   be able to chart the route of the Exodus from Egypt.
    d.   be able to write a paragraph summing up the day's lesson.

or (through demonstration)

    a.   be able to decorate a sukkah.
    b.   create a menorah.
    c.   recite the kiddush.

or (through reading)

    a.   read the Shema prayer.
    b.   read and translate the conversation between the teacher and student.

or (through games)
  a. participate in a Jeopardy Game.
  b. play Holiday Lotto.

The students should have to do something each day so that the teacher can document that learning is taking place, that each child was involved in the lesson, and that each child was an active participant in class. Many times, only the most outgoing child is noted. This is the child who will volunteer to answer questions or take part in the discussion. The child who sits quietly may also be learning, but unless the teacher has a method for feedback, she may never know if her lesson was truly effective. Students usually respond well to tests at the end of a unit, at midterm and at the end of the year if learning has occurred. This is one way of summing up concepts, facts and skills that have been presented in class. Testing is also another way to legitimize the school. The students should know that they must have achieved a certain level of knowledge before moving on to the next grade. Does this mean that a child will fail? Absolutely not! A child cannot fail at being Jewish. It is the teacher's role to help them see what they have learned and to provide ways for them to demonstrate it. A child should not be evaluated on just one test or paper. She should also be evaluated on class participation, projects, homework assignments, and reports in addition to tests.

We must also realize that as everyone learns differently, so do they show their knowledge in different ways. If a child cannot express herself well on paper, listen to her. Some children cannot perform well on written reports, but they can illustrate what they have learned. For example, the class is assigned reports on different aspects of Israel. The child who researches industry and products of Israel may choose to create a map of Israel spotlighting the subject rather than writing a report.

Sometimes children will not achieve the objectives during the school year. Make-up assignments and remedial work can be required. Students who are not proficient in Hebrew studies may need a tutor so that they may remain with their class the following year. Always keep in mind that religious education is not secular education. It is not a priority with most parents and students, but there should be established standards that must be met if bar/bat mitzvah and confirmation are to be achieved.

Let's return to the subject of testing, as this is one of the most widely used forms of evaluation. There are many things to consider when preparing tests. Ask yourself: What is the objective of the test? Do I want the students to parrot back certain facts and figures? Do I want to test for basic concepts? Do I want them to use resources to find information? Do I want them to take the material and do something more with it? Do I want to know if they have internalized the teachings? The teacher needs to know the answers to these questions before composing the first test question.

There are other things to consider when preparing a test. How much time will the teacher have to evaluate the papers? Does she have time to read essays? Will she choose short answers, fill in the blank, circle the correct answer, or true and false statements?

The teacher must construct a test that can be completed in a specific time period. What can be accomplished in fifteen minutes, a half hour, or a whole hour? The teacher should take care when constructing the test so that it will not be a device to "catch the students and show them up." The test can be used in a positive manner as a teaching technique. It is important to note the difference between these two concepts.

How do we "catch the students?" Use difficult questions that the teacher knows students will have trouble answering. Phrase questions in unfamiliar terminology. Use words like "never" and "always." Test for irrelevant information. Count off for testing skills such as writing T for TRUE when the directions state "write TRUE or FALSE." Count off for spelling and grammar when you did not teach these skills. Our concern should be with the child's ability to grasp the material taught and her ability to use it rather than on game-playing to keep the scores low.

Be aware that the purpose of testing should be to answer the question "Am I teaching and are they learning?" If you are teaching and they are learning, terrific! If the test results show that the answer is "no," then review the test and check for the following:

     a.   Did the test evaluate the materials covered in class?
     b.   Did the language of the test affect the results?
     c.   Were the directions clear and concise?
     d.   Did the students have enough time to complete the test?

Take the time to evaluate the test. Graph the answers. How many students missed each question? Were some questions missed more than others? If so, were the students absent on the days that the concepts were covered? Were the incorrect answers similar on each paper?

Review your findings: How did you teach that missed concept? Can you think of another way to approach the subject? Do you have time to reteach the concept? If it is the final test and you will not see the students again, can you insert the correct answer so that the student can learn the concept when she reviews the test? This is another way in which you can reteach the material. If the child missed a whole section of an exam, you may want her to retake that part again. Supply her with the learning materials, give her time to study, and let her retake that section. It is not necessary to retake the whole test if only one part was in error.

A test can be another opportunity to teach that which was not retained the first time around.

If a test comes back to a student with an X by the answer, the student may think, "Oh well, I missed it." Most students will not make the effort to find the correct answer. However, if the right answer is supplied, she may read it and this time it could be retained.

Please keep in mind that there have been volumes written on test construction and evaluation. The concepts presented here were chosen because they reinforce the objective of planning for success.

Let's turn our attention to the types of questions that are used on tests, keeping in mind the course objectives, time needed to take the test, and time needed to evaluate the results.

1. **CIRCLE THE CORRECT ANSWER.**

   The Holy Scriptures contains the Law, the Writings, and the Prophets. How many books are in these three sections?
   a. 29
   b. 30
   c. 39
   d. 40

This question defines and reviews the concept "Holy Scriptures" and then asks the student to recall information about it. The student does not have to use total recall as she is given a choice of four answers. The teacher can use an answer sheet that fits over the page with the correct answer space left open or a separate answer sheet for easy evaluating.

2. **TRUE OR FALSE.** Write T for TRUE or F for FALSE in the space provided. If a STATEMENT IS FALSE MAKE IT TRUE.

   ___a. Torah means the "Written Law"

   ___b. The story of Abraham is found in the book of Exodus.

This question asks the student to make a judgment. She has a 50/50 chance of answering this question correctly. However, when the student marks a statement false she is being asked to recall more information and to really distinguish between what is true and what is not. It in no longer a guessing game. Constructing the question for its maximum effect will require more time for evaluation.

3. **ORDERING.** Place the Five Books of Moses in the correct order as they appear in the Torah.

   Leviticus Deuteronomy Genesis Numbers Exodus

This question asks the students to place given information in proper sequence. It can be used for steps in performing rituals, placing events in order etc. A higher form of this question would be, **"List the five books of Moses in the correct order as they appear in the Torah."** Do not list the books for the student. This type of question requires more evaluation time as the student must write the answers.

4. **DIFFERENTIATING.** Place a (J) for Jacob or an (E) for Esau in front of each word or words that describe that person.

   ___hunter   ___married an idol worshipper
   ___mediator   ___sensitive
   ___worked 14 years for wife   ___cunning
   ___leader   ___favorite of mother
   ___hairy   ___favorite of father
   ___sold birthright

This question asks the student to distinguish concepts or traits and then to match them to a particular person. The students might then be asked to write a description of Jacob or Esau and discuss why one brother would be the better leader for the Jewish people. An answer key could be used to evaluate the first part.

5. **LISTING.** List two ways in which the Bible influences our lives today.

   a. _____

   b. _____

This question asks the student to recall information and to make a judgment. Information is not given. Boundaries are not established. The teacher should expect a wide gamut of answers. Evaluation will take more time than quick answers.

103

6. **WRITE A PARAGRAPH.** Choose one of the following stories and tell what lesson you have learned from it.
   a.   Abraham and the worship of idols
   b.   Abraham and the division of land
   c.   Abraham and the three strangers
   d.   Abraham and the destruction of Sodom and Gomorrah
   e.   Abraham and the sacrifice of Isaac

This question asks the student to choose a topic and to describe what she learned from it. Two children writing on the same topic may have learned totally different lessons. What insights did the children gain from the stories? Evaluation time will be lengthy. The teacher will have to make a wide range of judgments as to what is acceptable or totally off the mark. The answers will give her tremendous insight into how her teaching is being perceived.

7. **LOCATE:** Locate the following passages in the Bible and copy them in the space provided.

   Genesis 17:2_____

   Leviticus 19:9-10 _____

This question tests a specific skill. Can the child use the Bible? Can she use the Table of Contents? Does she know how to find chapter and verse? The teacher can use an answer key and skim the list for words to check for correctness.

8. **FILL IN THE BLANK:**

   The agreement that Abraham made with God is called (in Hebrew)

   _____.

This question asks for recall of a word. A higher form of this question would ask the student to define the word *brit* or to ask the student to describe the contents of the covenant. In the upper grades, the students could be asked to describe the implications of the covenant in the question, "Whose land is it?" when discussing modern Israel. Simple recall questions can be evaluated quickly with an answer key.

9. **MATCHING.** Match the achievements from column 1 with the person in column 2.

____ invented the polio vaccine	a. Samuel Gompers
____ wrote poem on Statue of Liberty	b. Henrietta Szold
____ began the Youth Aliyah Movement	c. Jonas Salk
____ helped create early labor unions	d. Albert Einstein
	e. Emma Lazarus

The students are asked to recall information in a specific context. Matching can be a matter of elimination. Therefore, it is necessary to have more entries in one column than the other. The statements can also contain key concepts. Each time the child reads the statements, she reviews the information and therefore, reinforces the concepts. This is easily evaluated with an answer key.

10. **ESSAY.** Write a paragraph describing the Torah. Include the outer dressing, the materials from which it is made and what you observe when it is unrolled.

This question asks for a description. Parameters are given so that the student knows what is requested. Had the question read, **Describe the Torah**, the student may have written about only part of the question and not what the teacher really wanted to test. It is important to state the question in clear language so that the students will answer the question correctly. This form of testing will require the longest period of time for evaluation.

Now that the student has taken the test, the teacher must evaluate it. Whenever a child turns in work, a project or a test, the teacher is obligated to evaluate it, comment on it, and return it to the student. Many times the teacher will just check that a student did the work. She will put a mark in her gradebook and throw away the paper. If the student does work, then she has the right to expect to see it graded and returned. This is the only way that the student can grow from the experience. She needs to see what she answered correctly and incorrectly.

When a student writes an opinion, a paragraph, or an essay, react to it. Let her know that you agree or disagree with her. Let her know if she needs more information, that her facts are incorrect, that she is entitled to her opinion and how it is similar to or different from mainstream Judaism. Use the assignment as a way to communicate more information or to reinforce her thinking. Let the child know that you appreciate her efforts, or that you really think that she could do better. Explain how she could do better.

Write what you see or feel:

"Jason, this was an excellent paper. Your reasons for observing Shabbat were right on target. Your experiences were rich and meaningful, and were helpful in creating a positive picture."

"Ellen, your list of Moses' problems in the wilderness was complete. Good job!"

"Eddie, you need to reread pages 12-14 in our text. Your information on Abraham and how he divided the land was confusing. Use the book and redo."

"I understand your feelings that 'love can conquer all,' but you are neglecting the reality of dealing with both sets of parents and your own future children if you choose to marry a person from another faith. Read the enclosed and think about what others have experienced."

When a student takes the time to write and express herself, it is incumbent upon the teacher to respond. A "grade" may communicate a level of acceptance or non-acceptance, but it does not communicate the details that are needed for real growth.

The teacher needs to decide how she will report the results of the student's work if there is not an established procedure in the school. Sometimes the teacher can choose her own method for class work, but must use the standardized school report card for communicating with parents. There are many grading systems that are used in secular and Religious Schools. These include using letter grades: A, B, C, D, or F, using percentage grades 100, 90, 80, 70, 60 or using a pass/fail.

What do we really want to accomplish when we report the results to students? We want the students to know that they did learn something—or that they missed the mark. We want them to know their strong areas and where they need to improve. We want to praise their efforts or let them know that they could have done a better job. Do we want to label them as "A" or "C" students? They do need to know about their progress in a subject area, but we must also let them know that we recognize their contributions to the class, their effort and their internalization of Jewish values as demonstrated through their actions in class. Do we want our students to leave us thinking and feeling that they are failures because they did not perform well on tests or other tasks? Realize that some of our students meet with failure in many other educational settings. We do not want the Religious School to be another place that reinforces their failure.

What can we do to see that this does not take place? In a school that stresses planning for success, we must also help our students feel successful. Each student should be encouraged to do her best. Sometimes this is not easy to do when the student puts forth little effort, but the investment is worth it.

EXAMPLE:

When I think back to my days of internship in a public school in Gainesville, Florida, I am reminded that sometimes a teacher must try unorthodox methods to facilitate a positive change in a child's life. Steve Voss, my internship teacher and mentor, demonstrated this to me.

I was sitting in the back of the room grading papers. Steve joined me and showed me James' report card which he had just completed. I looked at the grades and then at Steve. Something was wrong. The card contained mostly C's and maybe one or two B's. James did not deserve these grades. He usually made D's and F's and perhaps a few C's. This was the sixth grade and James was 14 years old. He had repeated sixth grade, as well as other grades. It looked as though he would never leave elementary school.

"How can you do this?" I asked. Steve explained that failing James had not worked. He had given up on himself years ago and had resigned himself to being a loser. He needed someone to believe in him, to let him know that he had value and that he could be successful. Steve was ready to be that person. He explained to me that two things could happen when James received the report card. He could think that the teacher was easy and a pushover and then continue on as usual or he could realize that someone cared and was giving him a chance to break the failure cycle.

The most amazing thing happened. When James received his report card, his face reflected puzzlement and then became all smiles. Beginning the next day, that child really worked. He changed right before our eyes. He paid attention in class. He did his homework. He asked for help when he needed it. His grades began to improve and when he received his next report card, it was truly representative of his efforts.

Steve had established a classroom where children, teacher, and intern would be successful. Everything that we did reflected this goal. Steve believed in James. Therefore, the child could risk believing in himself.

Most children will live up to our expectations. If we tell them that they can't do it, they won't. If we tell them they can, they will try. We must encourage children to set realistic goals and help them work towards them.

17.
EFFECTIVE COMMUNICATION WITH PARENTS

There are many ways in which teachers can communicate with parents. Schools may have established methods that must be followed. The teacher should become aware of these before the school year begins.

Parents want to know about their child's academic progress and about his behavior in class. Most schools use some type of report card system to convey this information to the parents. In most cases waiting until the official reporting period to report these items is acceptable. However if a child has poor attendance, is often tardy to class, misbehaves on a regular basis, is not participating is class or is not grasping the basic concepts then the parents need to know about this early in the semester.

Teachers can establish communication in many ways. Postcards may be sent home when a child is absent, indicating that the child was missed. If he has the materials at home, he can complete a make-up assignment, or the materials could be sent with the expectation that the work is due the following session. If a child is absent for two consecutive sessions, a phone call should be made to inquire into the child's health or other reasons for not being in school.

It is helpful if the school has an attendance policy in place and the administration has a means of following through.

Teachers should also follow up on multiple tardies to class. Sometimes parents bring their child to school on time, but the child is visiting with others or meandering in the halls. Parents want to know this. Sometimes parents need to be reminded that it is in the child's best interest to be in class at the appropriate time.

At times personal conferences are necessary. If these take place before class begins or after school time, they should occur so that they do not interfere with class time. These meetings should be conducted in a quiet place where you will not be interrupted by others.

Teachers also communicate through written notes. Some teachers send special messages when a child brings in extra projects, shares an interesting family happening, or does a mitzvah in class.

The most common form of communication with parents remains the report card. Some schools will send them home two or three times a year. It is important to note that a poor grade of "needs improvement" or "unsatisfactory" should never be given if the parents were not contacted during the grading period. When the grade is given without prior notice, the parents have every right to inquire as to why they were not notified earlier so that they could work with the child towards improvement.

Teachers need to make full use of the report card. Usually there is a place for teacher comments. Many times teacher will write comments that do not give insight into the child's class performance. These comments are useless.

Example:

Darren is a lovely child and a pleasure to teach.

Have a wonderful vacation.

Leah has shown progress this term.

Michael had a good year.

Report cards are sometimes a way to share negative feelings toward the child and his performance. This is damaging to the child and invites the parents to wonder why they were not contacted. It can also make the situation seem hopeless.

Example:

Steven did not do well on his test. He puts very little effort into his Religious School work.

Rachel is a poor Hebrew reader. She still does not know all of the letters and vowels.

Melissa socializes with her friends instead of paying attention to the lesson.
Joshua needs to participate more in group discussions.
Sam is uncooperative.

Students should never be compared to others in the class. Their progress should be judged on how they have improved from evaluation period to evaluation period. Students and parents discuss the report card with other students and their parents. Comparisons create hurt feelings.

Example:

Amy was my best student. She is so bright.
Barry scored lower than all the other students in the class. He must study more if he is to succeed.
Beth was my joy and pleasure. She was the top student in everything.

Comments should reflect the child's performance in class during the evaluation period. Both the negative and the positive should be reported. The teacher should be able to find something positive to say about every child. Some teachers say that this is not always possible. If this is so, then the parents and child should be given hope that what is now can change, and that together, by doing "X they can make it happen.

Example:

Tammy reads smoothly and is improving in accuracy. She has difficulty with self-control, but has lately shown a real effort to improve. I would like to see it continue.

Jennifer's commitment to Jewish values was evident in the way that she shared her knowledge and supplies with our new student.

David's report on anti-Semitism was outstanding. He made good use of picture material and held the interest of the class.

Benji contributes to all our class discussions and he asks excellent questions. He needs to listen when other students are participating. I know that this will improve.

Since we spoke Sammy is arriving on time. He is now ready when class begins. He has made many fine contributions to our class. He was an excellent group leader on our Bible Treasure Hunt.

Marla's erratic attendance impacts negatively on her class work and participation. It is very difficult to feel a part of the class when this happens. I am concerned about her progress. She is capable and I am sure that with more regular attendance she will excel in Religious School.

Teachers must find opportunities to communicate with parents. They will appreciate your concern and your feedback. When you have a problem, involve them into the solution. They know their child better than anyone. They know how he performs in secular school, in the family and in the neighborhood. They know what interests the child and what frustrates him. You need their help when aiming for success. Parents will be supportive and will cooperate. (For further information on communication with parents, see *Planning For Success* by Dorothy C. Herman, Torah Aura Productions.)

18.
USING IMMEDIATE
MOTIVATORS

There are many things that happen in our students' lives from week to week. We have so little time with them that we must find ways to draw them quickly into our academic world. Using an immediate motivator will help accomplish this. This technique is also helpful in curbing late starts in class due to student socializing and not settling down immediately. When students become accustomed to finding work at their desk or on the board as they come into the room, they realize that class has begun and they have a task to complete. While students are doing these assignments, the teacher can record absences, collect Keren Ami money, discuss a problem with an individual student, etc.

An immediate motivator can be an assignment reflecting previous lessons. For example: Write a newspaper article describing the Jews' arrival in New Amsterdam in 1654; or, write a letter to your mother telling her about life on the lower East Side in 1910; or, draw a picture of a family celebrating Hanukkah; or, complete the worksheet on Things I Will Need To Survive In The Wilderness With Moses. These activities can be completed in a short time.

An immediate motivator can be an assignment that prepares the student for the lesson of the day. For example: "Today we will join Moses and the Hebrews as they leave Egypt. List those things that you will need to take with you so that you can survive in the wilderness;" or, "Write a paragraph describing what you expect to see and experience when your ship lands

113

from Russia in America in 1905;" or, "Write a paragraph stating how you would like the class's Keren Ami money to be allocated and why."

19.
PARENTS AND STUDENTS LEARNING TOGETHER

Parents are an important part of teenagers' lives, though many teens would like to put space between themselves and the older generation. Parents tend to come to "school things" for younger children more readily than for their older offspring. I feel very strongly that parents should be involved in the learning process at all ages so that they can see firsthand how and what their children are learning. In a Religious School class they can also increase their own knowledge and better appreciate the excellent education that their child is receiving.

Keeping this in mind, every effort should be made to involve parents in the Religious School experience of teenagers. At Temple Beth Am parents are invited to the Monday Night Confirmation classes. This is not a time for assembled, informational meetings, or for observing the school in action. It is a time for parents and students to learn together. The teachers are instructed to create a lesson using their regular curriculum that will involve both generations. Parent night usually is scheduled for the fourth or fifth session of the trimester. This timing gives the teacher the opportunity to know the students and to become familiar with their learning styles.

20.
JEWISH LIFE AFTER CONFIRMATION: A COURSE CURRICULUM

The following is a selection of lessons, ideas, and strategies for success that I have used in my Confirmation class, *Jewish Life After Confirmation*. This material incorporates the concepts and methods discussed in the previous sections, and these will be highlighted here. I have been teaching this subject for over ten years. It is never the same because the students and our interaction are never the same. As a teacher and as a person, I grow and discover new ways to reach my class. Each year my students are different as individuals and as a group. Each class offers new challenges and new angles to the basic concepts that I want to transmit to the next generation.

Jewish Life After Confirmation is a course on life cycle. Each segment could take a semester, but I do not have that luxury. Our school year is divided into three 9 or 10 week trimesters. The last

117

session is reserved for the final exam. This leaves me eight to nine hours of teaching time, minus roll taking and tzedakah time. I guard my time the way a mother guards a baby. There is so much to teach and so little time. It forces me to be efficient. I have had to choose the most important concepts and delete others that I would have liked to include. I have had to sacrifice some of my favorite methodology in the process. But, I am not wedded to the written word. I am able to approach each semester with flexibility. Knowing that my students have not had a course in life cycle since fourth grade, I have chosen to focus on the areas of Confirmation, marriage and death, taking my students where they are and giving them background for what they will experience in the future.

I have included only part of the curriculum. The first few lessons are crucial to my plan for success. They set the ground rules, motivate participation, and build community. These are necessities with any class, grade level, or subject matter. The last two sessions of the course are concerned with Jewish death practices and rituals. By this time we must be a tight community so that the students are comfortable sharing their experiences with death and funerals.

Read this section carefully. You will find that the suggestions for success are illustrated in detail. These can be useful in helping the reader formulate her own philosophy and course of action.

SESSION ONE

OBJECTIVES:

The students will:
1. meet the teacher and hear the rules of the class and a description of the curriculum.
2. be able to list each others' names and begin building community in the classroom.
3. participate in an exercise in awareness.
4. preview their notebooks to discover the focus of the class.
5. complete a personal questionnaire.

SET:

The furniture is arranged in a semicircle (more eye contact, feeling for group, ease of move-ment). The teacher's name and the name of the course are on the chalkboard. As the students arrive, the teacher greets each one, makes contact and encourages them to sit within the semi-circle.

MEET THE TEACHER

1. The teacher welcomes the total class and tells them her name and that of the course, *Jewish Life After Confirmation*, and that we will be studying Confirmation, marriage and death rituals. She then calls the roll and begins the process of connecting names to students. Comments are made if the teacher remembers other children in the family. She then tells the students about herself. Information includes what the teacher does professionally, about her family, pets, likes and dislikes, and why she chose to be a part of the Jewish educational process.

2. The teacher should be positive about teaching the group and about the curriculum, but should also establish the class rules right away. (I like to tell my Confirmation classes that they are the icing on my cake. All week I work with the administrative problems of running a large school. I teach seminars for adults and write curriculum, but the favorite part of my job is teaching confirmands. Confirmation is special and I always look forward to the class. If the class has the reputation of being a good class, I tell them that I have heard good things about them and I know what super students they are. If they are a rough class, I tell them that I know that we are really going to have a great class and that we are going to learn a lot this semester. I tell them that I like to be happy when I teach. Therefore, I have rules that we will follow so that our time together will be pleasant.)

CLASS RULES:

(These make me happy because they work for me. Each teacher must find rules that work for her. Some teachers let the students help formulate the rules and the consequences for the class. In my particular setting and time frame, this is not feasible.)

A. Everyone must arrive on time. This includes the teacher.

Classes will not be lecture sessions. There will be some kind of teacher input during the first five or ten minutes. After that the students will be responding through discussion, writing, or doing. If the students miss the first few minutes then they will have difficulty during the rest of the hour and will not gain the full benefit of the class. If the carpool brings a student after class begins more than once, I call the driver and tell him of our rule. I feel **that** strongly about arriving for class promptly. (If students are permitted to drift into class, they will cause a disruption. They will not know what is going on. If the teacher waits for the students to arrive then she sends the message that the lesson is not important and it can wait.)

B.   Excessive talking is not permitted.

Usually in a class like this students will want to discuss side issues with their neighbors. The class can best be conducted if each person shares with the total group. When the teacher is talking, the students will not. When a student is talking, the other students will not. When a student is talking, the teacher and other students will give her their respect and attention. What a student thinks and says will be important in this class. I expect everyone to share.

C.   Chewing of gum is permitted as long as bubbles are not blown and the gum is not cracked. I do not want to see it or hear it. This is a privilege as long as it is not distracting. Other food and drinks may not be sold or eaten in class.

(Sometimes our students sell candy for secular school clubs or the Confirmation class sells snacks during the time between their two classes.)

D.   Secular work may not be done in class.

Many students will have exams the next day or may have assignments that are due. Our class is not a place to do other school work. I explain that what we will be doing is so important that they will not have time to think about anything else. We have less than an hour and we have so much to learn. I promise them that I will not bring in my other work either. I won't use our time to do school scheduling, my homework from the classes I am taking, or to fold my laundry. I will prepare to teach them and give them my full attention.

E.   Students must bring in a pen or pencil each week.

They will be required to write something each week. If they don't remember, I will lend them a pen, but if this occurs often they will have to give me something in return so they will remember the next time. (This is only for students who never remember. They give me a watch, necklace, or shoe which is returned at the end of class.)

F.   The students must pass the final exam.

This is an academic class needed for Confirmation. Most students do this without a problem. No one fails the test or the course. A student must retake that part of the test that is not mastered. Exams are mailed home to parents complete with comments on the test and about the student's performance in class.

G. Students are permitted one absence during the 10-week period. More absences require make-up work.

I will mail this to them the day after class. The student will complete it and return it to me at the next session. He will receive an assignment even the first time that he is absent. He does not have to do the written work, but he is responsible for the content. I put in this extra time because I really feel that what I teach is important and I want my students to know it. (I have found that most of my students complete the work and return it the next session without my even asking for it. Those who forget apologize when they realize that they erred and either mail it in or bring it the next session. There is an attitude of accepting responsibility.)

The students are given the opportunity to question the class rules and to respond to them.

BE ABLE TO LIST EACH OTHERS' NAMES...
PARTICIPATE IN AN EXERCISE IN AWARENESS

3. The next activity is an awareness exercise which I begin by saying the following:
    Now that we know what the rules are we can move on to tonight's lesson. We are going to take part in an exercise in awareness. Please remove everything from the top of your desk.

    I am going to give you something of value—a very special gift. When you receive it I want you study it, know it from every angle, feel it, and treasure it. It is of great value and though it may look as if it is the same as your neighbor's, it is not. Look careful- ly. Each one will be quite different and precious. Make it yours. Care for it. Do not change its appearance in any way.

The teacher has a bag containing leaves that have come from the same tree and are very similar in appearance. They are approximately the same size and shape with few distinguishing marks. The teacher takes one leaf at a time from the bag, and places one on the desk of each student. The students usually giggle when they see what is in the bag. They are reminded to study their leaves carefully and to really get to know them. Give the students a few minutes to do this.

Then place the students with their leaves in groups of four. Assign each group a different area of the room and have them sit on the floor. If you can remember their names, call them by name. Have them introduce themselves to each other, tell which school they attend, and what they like to do when they have free time. Tell them that they will have to know every- one's name at the end of class. (This is not necessary if you have a small school and everyone knows each other. We have 80 or more students in a grade level. Students could be in the

121

school for 10 years and not know everyone on their grade level as they could have been in different classes or attended on different days.) The students are instructed to place their leaves in a circle of four on the floor. One student (by name) is asked to pick up the leaves, mix them together without hurting them and then place them back on the floor. The students are told to retrieve their very own special leaves. If there is a problem in finding the right one, the student is given time to study the others' leaves so that she can find her own. The teacher should remember the comments that the students make at this time.

The groups should be rearranged. New groups are formed and the process repeats itself. This pattern can be followed:

A. first group of four

B. rearranged groups of four

C. rearranged groups of six

D. rearranged groups of eight

E. arrange two large groups of half the students

F. one large group of everyone

Always have the group introduce themselves and discuss something, e.g., favorite Jewish holiday, what they would do if they won the lottery, a mitzvah they have done. The teacher always appoints one person to mix the leaves. (Use the student's name even if you have to ask for it. This will help the teacher and students remember names.) The teacher should be observing behavior throughout this process. When the total group is in the circle, give them the opportunity to ask anyone in the group for their name. Then have all the students give their leaves to one student who will mix them up and place them in the middle of the circle. Each student is to retrieve her leaf and return to her original chair. When all of the students are seated, the teacher goes from student to student asking each how she knew that it was her leaf. The students explain that theirs had a bump or a dark vein or a spot that helped them identify their leaf. Sometimes the leaf will have acquired a name. The teacher keeps the students occupied with discussion of the leaf as she takes it away. If a student is reluctant to give up her leaf, keep on insisting. Most will part with it. (I have only had 4 students refuse to give it up. One student brought it to class for five sessions. It was finally thrown out by the maid when she was cleaning his room. Another student kept it the whole semester and had it with her on Confirmation morning.) The teacher then goes to the front of room, waits for everyone's full attention, smiles and tears the leaves into pieces.

There is usually an outburst or gasp. "Why did you do that?" "That was my leaf. You shouldn't have done that!" "Why did you give it to us and then tear it up?" "Why did you kill Fred?" The teacher waits until everyone is quiet. Then she tells the class that this was an Exercise in Awareness. "You have become aware of this wonderful gift that I gave you. You kept track of it through all kinds of movement and groups. Then, so easily, you gave it up and I was able to destroy it. It is gone forever. I didn't have to work very hard to take this precious gift away from you. I guess you didn't value it enough. Now, I want you to do some really deep thinking and to become aware of what this all really means. What did the leaf represent to you? What is an important concept or thing in your life that you would be willing to fight to retain? Who or what would I have represented that could take your thing of value away from you?"

The teacher writes two column headings on the chalkboard, A. SOMETHING OF VALUE and B. TAKER. Each student is called upon to place items in each column. In column A the students list things like family, friends, life, dog, car, freedom, religion, etc. In column B, they list fire, cults, war, a thief, dictator, drugs, death, government, etc. We discuss how the two columns interact, the effect that they have on each other and on us, and how we can "fight back" and hold on to those things that are meaningful to us. We discuss really valuing that which we have and realizing how easily things can really be taken from us.

Specific students are asked specific questions where they fit. "How did you feel when you couldn't find the right leaf?" "Why did you let David have your leaf when you knew it was yours?" (You didn't care enough. The gift didn't matter.) "You said that the leaf represented your family. Would you let your family go that easily?" "Why did you let me take your leaf? You began to challenge me, but then you backed down. Why? What value or thing would you really be willing to fight for?" "What did we learn about ourselves and what we value from this exercise?"

I sum up the exercise by saying:

We must become aware of what matters to us, what we value. Sometimes we don't realize how much we value something until it is gone. Each new day is a gift, just like our
leaf. It is up to us to decide what we want to do with this gift...use it, cherish it, waste it.
This course is going to deal with things of value...Jewish values. This is a gift that your
parents are giving to you by sending you to this school. We have taught you our history,
rituals, and ethics. Some of you value these gifts. Some of you do not. My role this
semester is to help you to study your leaf of Judaism. If you really know it and value it,
then no one can take it away from you. It will enrich your life and it will become a part of
you. Each session I will give you a leaf. It will be drawn on the board with our topic for the
evening in it. You will learn to love some of these leaves. You will cherish them and they

123

will become a part of you. Others you will reject. This is part of being a confirmand...
studying our tradition and choosing those aspects of it that are meaningful to you.*

4. The students are then given a questionnaire (page 125) to complete. The students are
    told that the teacher needs to know more about them so that the lessons will reflect
    their needs and level of knowledge. No one will see these papers other than the teacher.
    As the teacher hands each student a paper, each student is asked to tell one thing that
    she learned about the teacher in class tonight. (This is a high-risk exercise as there is no
    guarantee what the students will say. This exercise gives the teacher the opportunity to
    learn how the students are perceiving her and to ascertain whether they are really listen-
    ing.) The students usually say of me: has four sons, worked at the temple for a long time,
    loves teaching, has rules, owns a Doberman, likes to make us think, wants us to learn, is
    very serious about the course, makes learning interesting, takes leaves away, etc. Do the
    students seem challenged? Do the students seem positive or negative towards the
    teacher and the class? Has their interest been aroused or do they feel threatened?
    Handle negative comments carefully. Be aware of areas where students have negative
    comments and temper your attitude and delivery.

    The students are also given an envelope to address to their parents. They are told that the
    teacher will communicate at least two times with parents during the semester. The first let-
    ter (see page 126) will tell about the course, its requirements, and readings the parents can
    do. A course outline will also be sent. The second communication will be the final exam
    and report card.

    As the students complete the questionnaire, they are given their workbooks. They will
    become familiar with the course and will have something constructive to do while the oth-
    ers are working.

5. The session ends with students volunteering to name all of the others in class including the
    teacher.

---

* Adapted from "Parable" by Neal S. Federman, *Alternatives in Religious Education*, Winter, 1974

QUESTIONNAIRE

Jewish Life After Confirmation

My name is _____

I have been attending Religious School_____years.

I think of myself as a _____ Jew.

I am getting confirmed because_____

At Confirmation I will be reaffirming the following beliefs or values: _____

_____

I need to know the following about Judaism which no one has taught me yet: _____

_____

When I think of getting married in the future, I keep the following in mind: _____

_____

My reaction to interfaith marriage (example: Jew/Christian) is _____

When I think of marriage and having children, I _____

When the subject of death comes up, I _____

_____

I need answers to the following questions on the subject of death and Judaism:_____

_____

NOTE: *A questionnaire can be created to reflect another curriculum.*
(Example Comparative Religion)
When I hear the word Jesus, I think_____
I need to know the following about Jewish God beliefs: _____

(Example Holocaust)
When I hear the word Holocaust, I _____
My reaction to the Holocaust is _____

Dear Parents,

Your tenth-grader will be in my class, *Jewish Life After Confirmation* for this term of Monday Night School. During this time, we will explore three main areas: Confirmation, Marriage, and Death. Please read the enclosed outline and questionaire that your child received at our first meeting. This will help you visualize our direction and will give you the opportunity to discuss the course with your child.

The purpose of this course is to give the student basic knowledge of Reform Jewish practices and the reasons behind them so that they will be able to confront decisions that will be theirs to make in the next few years. The Jewish point of view will be presented.

We will not be using a basic text, but instead a variety of materials and methodology. These will include videos,role playing, awareness exercises, decision making, discussion, lectures, readings and listing exercises. Your child will miss a tremendous amount of input if he\she is absent. Reading and written assignments will be necessary to make up class work missed.

It is important that the student is in class on time as we begin promptly with group motivation. The students know the class rules and are expected to follow them at all times. To receive Confirmation credit for this course, the student must pass the final exam, which when completed and evaluated will be mailed to you.

The following books are available to you in our library if you wish to further your knowledge:

1. *Liberal Judaism at Home,* Bial.

2. *The Jewish Home,* Syme, U.A.H.C.

3. *The Jewish Catalog,* Book I and II, Strassfeld and Siegel

I thoroughly enjoy teaching this course and look forward to a great trimester with your student. If you wish to discuss your child, the curriculum, etc., with me, I am in the Religious School office Mondays through Wednesdays, 666-2536.

Sincerely,

Dorothy C. Herman, RJE
Director of Religious Education

SESSION TWO

PREPARATIONS:

The second session the students know what is expected of them. They will usually follow the rules from the previous week if they are stated in an acceptable way. I have found that if a student comes in late, he or she will give a reason and be apologetic as opposed to coming in and joining the class or coming in and disturbing the class. To continue stressing the building of community ask one student to name each student in the class. I remind them that I am a member of the class also and I want my name included.

Roll is formally taken if the teacher cannot remember all of the names, but as soon as possible this procedure is eliminated. Knowing each student by name is important. A student should be asked to tell the others one rule of the class. Again names should used. "Debbie, tell David one rule of our class." "Andy, tell Sam about the rule that deals with gum." Using this strategy, the teacher is not telling the rules, but the students are reminding or instructing each other. By using students' names in this procedure the teacher is reinforcing the need to know others' names.

The students are given their workbooks and asked to put their names and class period on the cover. It is explained that these workbooks are theirs to use in class. Each week when they come in they should pick them up from the teacher's desk, use them, and return them at the end of the session. Each week they will need a pen or pencil (reinforcement from the previous week). The students may write notes to the teacher, ask questions, or comment on the lesson. This will be a way in which we can communicate with each other. Sometimes a student will want to write about doubts, fears or questions that they may not want to share with the total class. The teacher can use the notebook to encourage a student, give a progress report, comment on absences, suggest that behavior needs to be improved, etc. The students look for the comments each week and question their absence if, heaven forbid, the teacher did not have time to read them. The students are told that the workbooks will remain at school until the week prior to the final exam. Then each student may use her own workbook for study purposes, but not as an open book for the test. In all of the evaluations the students said that these booklets were very helpful to them in organizing their thoughts and for studying for their final.

The students are given a few minutes to look at the outline of the course and at some of the activities in the workbooks. They are encouraged to ask questions about the curriculum. The workbooks set the tone for the course. The students now see that the course is very well organized. There is a body of material that they will be expected to learn. They see where the course is going and what they will learn. They know that the time spent in this class will not be wasted. They realize that they will have to produce each week. They cannot just sit in class like bumps on a log. They will have to participate.

OBJECTIVES:

1. The students will explore their Jewish beliefs and will be able to verbalize those that have meaning for them.

2. The students will search for their concept of God.

SET:

A leaf is drawn in the corner of the chalkboard each week. This session the word BELIEF is written in it. The symbol is pointed out to the students.

> "Tonight we will begin our unit on Confirmation. How many of you have had the opportunity to attend out temple's Confirmation service in the past? What do you remember about it? Why do we have Confirmation? What is its purpose?" (These questions are explored. It is a way of finding out what the students know in general about the life cycle event.)

PROCEDURE:

The teacher tells the class that Confirmation is that time when we stand before our family and our congregation and we reaffirm our beliefs in Judaism that we have right now. What we believe will change with knowledge, maturity and age, but Confirmation is that time when we really try to clarify what we believe and not what our parents, rabbis, and teachers believe.

> To begin, say something like, "Pam, pretend that you are a freshman at the University of Florida and are rooming with two roommates from small towns who have never really met a Jew before. They ask you to explain what it means to be a Jew. What do you tell them?" Pam has been put on the spot. She probably feels uncomfortable. Try to draw her out. Write her responses on the board. She may answer, "We believe in one God." "We have a Torah." "We have holidays." Whatever the responses, probe a little more. "What do you mean by one God?" "What do you believe about God?" "How does this belief affect your life?" or "What is a Torah?" "What is in it?" "Do you follow what is in it?" "What is your favorite part?" or "What holidays do you observe?" "Which one do you like best?" "How does you family celebrate it?"

> Include other students in similar situations. "Joey, you are an intern in a Baptist community. Some of your fellow interns have never met a Jew before. What do you say when they ask you, 'What is a Jew?' Lisa, you are on the debate team for your high school and travel to many other cities to compete. What do you say when asked about your beliefs?" Call on as many students as possible. List all of the answers on the board. Some will say, "My beliefs are already listed." Ask that student to explain what that belief means to her personally. Is her concept the same or different from Pam's?

128

This exercise involves each student. They realize that each one will be called upon and so they are both listening to others and doing some deep thinking about their own beliefs. The students may become uncomfortable. This is okay. They are beginning to wrestle with their own beliefs and what they really mean. They are becoming aware of the beliefs of their class-mates. It is easy to say, "I believe in the Ten Commandments." It is harder to answer, "Which commandment is the most meaningful one to you and how does it influence your life?"

The students are told that people of other faiths have to verbalize what they believe also. Have them listen carefully as the teacher reads the Nicene Creed. This is what Catholic children learn in their Religious School classes. Have them list what a Catholic believes. This can be done by asking each student to name one thing with the teacher writing it on the board or by having each student make a list. (This is done after the reading and not during. Students are lis-tening and remembering. Everyone is focused on the task.)

The students are asked what they learned from this exercise. Catholics have a stated creed that they profess. Do Jews have a creed? Usually, someone will eventually mention the Shema. Can we all agree that this is central to Judaism? They usually agree that it is, but in discussion we discover that not everyone can profess a belief in God or they are not really sure what they believe at this time. This is okay. It is good to be a searcher. This is what Confirmation is all about—a time to discover, put together, dig for beliefs. It is a time to become more knowledge-able.

NOTE: *The above exercise focused the students on the topics of Confirmation and personal belief. It was structured to emotionally involve each student and to bring each student into the lesson. Each was called on at least two times (own beliefs and questioned about them and what they remember from the Nicene Creed). They become uncomfort-able because they cannot parrot back what they have heard others say in the past or what they think the teacher wants to hear. They have to take ownership for their statements and explain them. Usually they have not had to do this in other classes. They should begin to feel the need for more knowledge. This usually works as a super motivator.*

Another variation could be to create a paper listing all of their responses to "At Confirmation I will be reaffirming the following beliefs or values:" from the questionnaire filled out the first session. Do not list who wrote them. Have the students read them and verbalize what the class will be reaffirming. Usually the responses are very general and at times weak. (See page 137.) List these on the board. Ask if we all can agree with each statement. Why? Why not? Is there anything that we can all say that we believe? This is another way to lead into verbalizing our beliefs.

Another strategy for stimulating thought and discussion on personal belief is to have the stu-dents complete the God Beliefs worksheet found on page 138. Some students will not be able to give a definite answer and they will want to place their checkmarks between the two columns. This is okay. When the students finish this page, they are asked to turn to another page in their notebook and write a paragraph summing up their God beliefs. Students are encouraged to share their paragraphs with the class, but no pressure is applied. Classmates may not challenge each other's beliefs at this time. This is a time for exploration and everyone should feel that the classroom is a safe place to search.

Sharing a personal story of your own lets the students know that others have also been uncomfortable with the search for a belief system and the ability to articulate it. I tell my students this one:

> Many times we go through years of Religious School without really wrestling with our beliefs, and we must do so if we are to grow. A few months after my own Confirmation, when I was 16, I was visited by my neighbor's son who had been away at college. I thought it was a friendly visit. He was handsome and I was flattered that he wanted to spend some time with me. We spoke about school, friends, etc. , but soon the conversation turned to the Bible and the New Testament. I knew that what he was telling me was in direct opposition to what Judaism taught, but I was unable to answer statements as to how and why the Jewish Bible foretold the coming of Jesus. I sat there, newly confirmed, feeling mighty dumb. Then he told me that he was in divinity school and that he would be preaching at the local church that night and he would like me to go with him, his parents and my Jewish friend that lived on our block.

> That night my friend and I sat through the church service, heard the fire and brimstone preaching of our neighbor, and watched many people come forward to be saved. We felt very uncomfortable. He called me the next day to invite me to come hear him preach again on Friday evening. I politely told him that it was impossible as I had to go to Temple that night.

> That experience had a profound effect on me, for I had been attending Religious School since third grade and I couldn't explain a thing about my religion when I was under pressure. I vowed to myself that I would never feel that inadequate again. I began attending adult education class and Shabbat services.

> Six years later, I had my first public school teaching position. (I had been working in a Religious School since high school). I was in a small country school in the middle of Florida. There were only four classes. The principal taught the seventh and eighth grade and was the community's Methodist minister. When he tried to convert me, I no longer felt inadequate. When he quoted chapter and verse, I was able to quote and interpret my own chapter and verse. It was a great feeling. I knew who I was and I could talk about it.

This is what I want for my students. I tell them,

> "You are Jewish. This is what you are. It is important for you to be able to verbalize your beliefs not only for others, but for yourself. During this class, we took an important step.

130

We have begun the search for ourselves. (We used one of the strategies stated in this section to stimulate discussion.) Each week we will take more steps. Hopefully, at your Confirmation you will be able to stand before our entire congregation and declare comfortably who you are as a Jew."

NOTE: *The students relate to personal stories. They become aware of the struggle that the teacher experienced and they begin to feel more comfortable about the growth process.*

At this point I give the students their responses to "At Confirmation I will be reaffirming the following beliefs and values:" from the *Jewish Life After Confirmation* questionnaire they filled out during the first session. These responses serve as motivation for a discussion on Jewish beliefs.

At Confirmation I will be reaffirming the following beliefs and values:

1. a family and trying to be a good Jew.
2. that I am Jewish and not some other religion or a Jew that doesn't care.
3. I believe in one God. I value the Torah and Bible.
4. I am a good Jew. I have followed my religion to the best of my ability.
5. I am proud to be a Jew.
6. Tzedakah, family, importance of keeping Judaism alive—education, kindness to all fellow men/women.
7. Those of the Jewish people.
8. Religious beliefs and values, life values.
9. Torah and God—be good and kind to all people.
10. Jewish morals and belief in tradition.
11. I am a Jew—Israel is really cool—I have been confirmed.
12. Be a good Jew—appreciate Judaism.
13. About my life, my beliefs as a Jew and holding them as mine.
14. The special traditions of the Jews.
15. Judaic laws—beliefs of family and friends.
16. That I am a Jew—I know about Judaism.
18. Even if I don't want to admit it, I respect my mother's religious feelings.
20. I am proud to be a Jew.
21. Understanding the meaning of the Jewish holidays.

GOD BELIEFS

From Howard Wasserman, Ellen Z. Charry, Diane King, Jerome Ruderman, eds., *Idea Cookbook* (Philadelphia: Board of Jewish Education, United Synagogue of America, 1976).

	YES	NO
1. I believe that God created the world and directs the happenings in it.	___	___
2. I believe that God has no power to interfere in the affairs of people.	___	___
3. I believe that the world came into being by accident.	___	___
4. I believe that God is aware of what I do.	___	___
5. I believe that God can answer prayer.	___	___
6. I believe that God punishes evil.	___	___
7. I believe that God intended us never to understand certain things about the world.	___	___
8. I believe that my concepts about God differ from the Torah's concept of God.	___	___
9. I believe that even if there were no people, God would still exist.	___	___
10. I believe that God decided what is good and what is evil.	___	___
11. I believe that God gets involved in human affairs when God wants to.	___	___
12. I believe that God rewards good.	___	___
13. I believe that God exists independently of, and outside of people.	___	___
14. I believe that prayer is an attempt to talk to God.	___	___
15. I believe that the Torah is the word of God.	___	___
16. I believe that God listens to prayer.	___	___
17. I believe that "God" is a term that people use to describe their best hopes for humanity.	___	___
18. I believe God exists only inside of people.	___	___
19. I believe that praying can benefit the person who prays, even if God doesn't listen.	___	___
20. I believe that "God" is an idea people use to describe those things beyond human understanding.	___	___
21. I believe prayer can have an effect on people's lives regardless of what they think about God.	___	___

What else do you believe about God? (Write your answer on the back.)

SESSION THREE AND FOUR

PREPARATIONS:

The leaf is drawn on the board with a question mark in it. Across the top of the board, in bold print write, YOU SHALL BE HOLY FOR I, THE LORD YOUR GOD, AM HOLY.

Students are always greeted by name as they come into the room. If the teacher feels that the class still does not know each other's names, one student could be called upon to name everyone.

By this time the teacher should have noted if certain students need to be separated. As the students come in, quietly and without embarrassing a student, the teacher can whisper that it might be a good idea for that student not to sit by a chatty friend. The student usually complies. If questioned, the teacher may tell the student that the visiting during class is distracting to the teacher and others and that we will try sitting the new way this class period. After class the teacher and student can discuss the situation and whether it is possible to have self-seating. A teacher should become aware of situations quickly and should handle them swiftly. If we give students "one more chance" and "one more chance," then the teacher is no longer in control. It is necessary to stop unacceptable behavior as soon as possible. This does not mean that the teacher pounces on every situation, every side conversation, but she must be aware of the effect behaviors are having on the class.

If the students completed work in their notebook and the teacher has read it during the week, she should comment on their efforts. They should be encouraged to keep up the good work. They should be reminded that the teacher reads each contribution and writes comments. The students can read these and write back if they wish.

OBJECTIVES:

The students will:
1. take an active role in decision making.
2. make value judgments and defend their decisions.
3. research values in Leviticus 19.
4. write two paragraphs based on their new insights.
5. discuss Jewish law.

SET AND PROCEDURE:

There is a leaf on the chalkboard with a **?** on it. Across the top of the chalkboard is written "Ye shall be holy for I the Lord your God am Holy." The teacher tells the class this session they will discuss and take part in the decision-making process. Part of being a confirmand is to begin making decisions about how we are going to live our lives. Ask students to think for a minute about who or what helps them to make decisions?

The teacher calls on different students. Usually their answers include parents, friends, brothers, sisters, teachers, counselors. These are listed on the board. As each one is named the student is also asked to name one decision that this person helped him to make. (Parent—what school to go to. Sister—which courses to take. Friend—what to wear.) This is followed by the question, "Why did you follow this person's advice?"

Pointing to the list, the teacher continues, introducing the next activity this way:

> All of these people plus many more influence what you do—the media (movies, television, magazines) will also influence what you will wear and buy and will introduce you to lifestyles different from your own.

> Each day you make hundreds of decisions. Some of them you never even think about. You just automatically do them—getting up in the morning at a certain time, getting out of bed on a particular side of the bed, which foot goes onto the floor first. Other things you really think about before you decide what to do—what to wear, to skip a class, who to eat lunch with. Decisions, decisions—all day long.

> During this class we are going to experience an exercise in decision making. As we do this, think of who or what influenced you to make your decision. Listen carefully. I have seven cards. Each card contains a problem or situation (page 144). They are real. They have happened to me or someone I know. We had to deal with it. I will ask for volunteers to pick a card. If we don't have volunteers, I will volunteer people. You will choose a card and read it aloud immediately. Do not take time to read the card to yourself first. Read it and then react to the situation on the card. Only the reader can talk. Everyone else must be quiet. When the reader is finished, then anyone can give an opinion. You may agree or disagree with each other.

At this point, a student may be asked to restate the rules. This will let the teacher know if students are listening. The class will pay closer attention the second time because emphasis is being put on the information. They may also wonder if they might be called on to restate the rules and they will want to know what to say.

NOTE: *During this exercise, the teacher does not give value judgments on anything that is said. The teacher may question and ask for clarification.*

When each card has been read and discussed the teacher then calls attention to the list of advisors previously listed on the board. When I teach this class, I continue this way:

> Throughout this exercise we spoke about what influenced our decisions. We said that these people helped us to make decisions. I would like to share with you something that

134

has helped me in my decisions. Last week I told you about my neighbor who took me to church. I made a decision then not to be dumb about my religion. I decided to read the Bible from cover to cover. Of course, I never quite did it, but I did make a start. Somewhere along the way, I read a part of the Bible that had a great impact on me and has truly influenced my life and my decisions as to how I would live and how I would interact with others.

The first night of class I told you that each week I was going to give you a leaf and that some of these you would love and want to keep, and about others you would say, "Sorry, that leaf is not for me." Tonight's leaf is one about which I hope you will say, "Hey, this is great. I want to take it with me."

Use a similar lead-in, and then erase the question mark in the leaf on the board. The word "Torah" is then written in it. Bibles are distributed and the students are asked to turn to Leviticus 19. They are not told the page number. Most of them, if they have been in our school from the middle grades, should know how to use a Bible. A neighbor will help them if they have trouble. A student reads the first paragraph. (Oh, that is what is written on the board.) Another is asked to explain its meaning. (God is holy, and we are expected to imitate this holiness.) "What does it mean to be holy?" (To act as God would, to behave in a certain way.) "How do we know what God wants us to do? We are going to find out."

Ask students to open their notebooks to the correct page, which has verses from Leviticus 19, the Holiness Code. Have students take a few minutes to write the verse or part of the verse indicated. Then they are to match up the situations that have been discussed from the cards (listed at the bottom of the notebook page) to the verses at the top. When they have completed this page, they turn to the next page in their notebooks and summarize their findings.

NOTE: *This exercise usually takes two sessions to complete. Bibles are on the desks at the start of the following session so that as soon as the students arrive, they pick up their notebooks and complete the assignment. (This technique of having work at their desks when students arrive helps to settle them into a serious mind set immediately. The work reminds them of the content from the previous week. It is built-in motivation.)*

When everyone has completed the writing, students are called upon to read each verse and match it to the situation card. The teacher helps to interpret the meaning of each verse and gives insight into these laws from other sources.

The students are then asked to turn to Rabbi Herbert Baumgard's "Basic Jewish Ideas", in their notebooks, and one is asked to read number three aloud. Then all are asked to read it to themselves and to really concentrate on the words and meaning. Discussion follows. What does this really mean? Is our world a stable place? What are some of the indications that the world is not stable? How do you feel about going out alone at night on a dark street? How do we have to protect ourselves and our families? How stable is a world living with the threat of nuclear war, hunger, drugs, teen-age suicide, and cults? What does this statement really say?

Using student responses we summarize the discussion. "If the world is built on Torah, then we will have a more stable world and people will be happier. One way we can work towards this more stable world is to know the law. It is the teacher's job to teach the law. The students' job is to study it...like you studied your leaf. Then decide if it is for you. Sometimes it is easier and more fun not to follow the law, but realize the consequences. If we want to enter into a partnership in making our world a better place then we must continue to learn the law and follow it. This is what Confirmation is all about."

Students have the option to read to the class their summaries of what they learned about the Bible and decision making.

NOTE: *The usual response is that the students did not realize that the Torah could give them guidance in decision making. They now realize that people in biblical days had the same problems that we have today and that they all can benefit from knowing the law. Some students want to learn more about Jewish law and we have brought in copies of the 613 commandments for study along with other source material. The students begin to realize that becoming confirmed brings responsibility and the need for knowledge.*

ANOTHER NOTE: *This method of exposing students to Torah has been very effective. It provides a way to take the student where he is, with problems that are real to him, and to link him to the writings and wisdom of our people. This works far better than, "Tonight we are going to study Leviticus 19. Please open your Bible."*

VALUE CARDS

NOTE: *Student response is very interesting to these situations.*

EXAMPLE: The discussion of the situation that involves the money from the discount store usually includes responses such as: "They try to rip you off in that place, so they deserve what they lose." "If it was a small boutique where you know the people and they are nice to you, you take it back." "If they are so dumb, they deserve to lose it." "But, the cashier will have to pay it out of her salary when the register is off." "Stealing is stealing." "They certainly wouldn't come out to the parking lot looking for me if they didn't give me enough money." "That happened to me when I was working and I appreciated the person returning the money."

EXAMPLE: The situation involving the president of the AZA and the pregnant sweetheart usually finds many of the students horrified that you should repeat something that you weren't supposed to hear in the first place. Others just have to tell at least one friend, who of course, would tell one friend. Some would confide in parents because if you really have to tell someone, they would be the safest persons to tell.

VALUE CARDS	Your father gives you $10 to buy gardening supplies at a discount store. When you get out in the parking lot you realize that the cashier has given you change for a twenty. What do you do?
You overhear a conversation between the president of a rival AZA group and the sweetheart. She frantically tells him that she is pregnant and doesn't know what to do. Your group is meeting that night. Do you tell your friends?	There is a big one-day sale at Burdine's. Your favorite jeans are half price. You arrive at the mall, and the sky is blackening with an oncoming storm. The only parking places that are available are two handicapped spaces near the entrance to the store and spaces at the very end of the lot. What will you do?
Your parents and the Greens have had a bitter disagreement. They had been in business together, but after accusations of stolen money and mismanagement the partnership dissolved. They do not speak to each other. You go to camp for the summer and the Greens' child is in your cabin. You will be together for the next four weeks. What will you do?	New neighbors move in next to your home. They are from Jordan. The father will be teaching in the language department at the university. They have a child your age. Will you be friendly, introduce him to your friends at school and try to help him adjust to America?
You are walking down the street when all of a sudden a big teenager comes out of a doorway. He grabs the purse of an elderly woman and knocks her to the ground. He runs away. What do you do?	You baby-sit for the Danbys every week-end. You use the money to pay for gas and up-keep on your car. You need the money. Lately Mrs. Danby has not been paying you at the end of the evening. She says that she does not have the correct amount or that she needs to change big bills. She does pay you, but sometimes it is much later in the week. What do you do?

EXAMPLE: The situation involving the handicapped parking finds the students in total agreement. They would never park in the space even if it meant missing the sale or driving around for a while until a space became available. Television commercials, the fear of a stiff fine and compassion helped in the decision making process.

JEWISH LIFE AFTER CONFIRMATION

"YE SHALL BE HOLY FOR I, THE LORD YOUR GOD, AM HOLY"

Using the Bible: Leviticus 19

Write the following verses.

_____1.   Leviticus 19:11

_____2.   Leviticus 19:13 (second part)

_____3.   Leviticus 19:14

_____4.   Leviticus 19:16 (first part)

_____5.   Leviticus 19:16 (second part)

_____6.   Leviticus 19:18

_____7.   Leviticus 19:34

Match each of the following situations with the biblical verse listed above that would apply to it by placing the letter in the space before the number of the verse.

        A.   Purse Snatcher

        B.   Baby Sitter

        C.   The Camp

        D.   Discount Store

        E.   Neighbor From Jordan

        F.   Parking At Burdine's

        G.   Sweetheart Pregnancy

1.   I learned the following about decision-making: _____

_____

2.   I learned the following about the Bible _____

_____

BASIC JEWISH IDEAS

by Rabbi Herbert M. Baumgard, D.H.L.

While Judaism is the evolving and changing religious expression of the Jewish people, Jews have always believed a basic core in all ages. Certainly, the core of our belief as understood by Reform Judaism is as follows:

1. GOD IS ONE—that is, there is one plan and purpose for the universe; there are no conflicting wills; no good god competing with a devil; nor are there greater and lesser gods or divine beings.

2. THE NATURE OF THIS GOD IS TO BE UNDERSTOOD IN TERMS OF CREATION, LAW, JUSTICE, MERCY, FORGIVENESS, LOVE—that is, He is not a blind force, acting on sudden whim, nor is He angry and punitive (this understanding of the nature of God evolved over thousands of years and is open to new insights). God is not to be understood in terms of human powers or definitions and is beyond man's full comprehension.

3. THERE IS A TORAH, A MORAL LAW, UNDERGIRDING THE UNIVERSE, AND MAN'S HAPPINESS AND THE STABILITY OF SOCIETY DEPEND ON THE LEARNING AND OBSERVANCE OF THIS LAW.

4. A MAN'S RELIGIOSITY IS TO BE DEDUCED FROM HIS ACTIONS, NOT FROM HIS STATED BELIEFS. (CONDUCT, NOT PROFESSED FAITH, IS THE CRITICAL MATTER.)

5. MAN IS BORN WITH THE POTENTIAL TO BE GOOD OR EVIL DEPENDING UPON HIS OWN CHOICE TO FOLLOW THE MORAL LAW. He is not born in "original sin," nor need he be mystically or miraculously "saved" from this "sin." Hence, the notion of the growth and improvement in the character of man by creating the good society becomes possible.

6. THIS WORLD IS THE CENTER OF MAN'S EXISTENCE. Whatever the "world to come" may be, man must correct the evil in this world. "It is not incumbent upon him to finish the task, but neither is he free to neglect it."

7. MEN MUST STRIVE TOWARDS A MESSIANIC DAY, WHEN ALL MEN SHALL LIVE IN PEACE AND HARMONY. There is a meaningful future ahead which men must strive to achieve with God's help. There is a part of the Messiah in all of us, and we must bring the pieces together to create "God's Kingdom."

8. MAN IS A CO-PARTNER WITH GOD IN THE CREATION THAT KNOWS NO END. God frequently relies on man to serve as His agent, and man must understand his responsibility. "Where there are no men...be thou the man."

9. JEWS ARE BOUND TO GOD IN A SPECIAL COVENANT OR AGREEMENT. Since they were the first to proclaim the idea of one God and one mankind, since they were the first to proclaim the moral law, they have a special responsibility to be exemplary in character and to teach these ideas, by example, to the world.

The following activities are used after the Decision Making activity in my Confirmation class to capture the students' attention and to reinforce what we have studied. They do one each week at the beginning of the session. Each student completes it individually and then the total class discusses the concepts. They continue to realize that the Torah is relevant to this day.

Read this Letter to Ann Landers:

Dear Ann,

This morning, when I pulled into a parking lot, a woman directly in front of me drove her car into a space marked with a two-foot-high sign that read, "Handicapped Parking Only."

I politely asked her if she had seen the sign. She snarled, "Yes, but I'm in a hurry."

How can people be so inconsiderate? Don't they realize it's extremely difficult for a person in a wheelchair or on crutches to shop when he must park several blocks from the store? Could I have made a citizen's arrest?

Boiling in Dubuque

Paraphrase a verse from Leviticus 19 that applies to this situation.

_____

_____

_____

_____

_____

_____

THE SNAKE THAT POISONS EVERYBODY

It

topples governments,

wrecks marriages,

ruins careers,

busts reputations,

causes heartache, nightmares,

indigestion,

spawns suspicion,

generates grief,

dispatches innocent people to cry

in their pillows.

Even its name hisses.

It's called gossip.

Office gossip. Shop gossip. Party

gossip.

It makes headlines and headaches.

Before you repeat a story, ask yourself—

Is it true?

Is it fair?

Is it necessary?

If not,

Shut up.

Paraphrase a verse from Leviticus 19 that applies to the lines above. _____

_____ _____

_____

_____

SUPPOSE IT WERE YOU

BEATEN, ROBBED:

Her real pain is no one cared.

Sidelights of a City:

Are we too calloused by violent crime to care any more?

Sgt. George Kent, Metro police: "Another mugging, and who gives a damn? People are so conditioned that they don't respond any more. Someone should have at least gone to my wife and said, 'Hey can we do something? Can we get a doctor?'

"No. They let her lie there, like a piece of paper in the wind…"

It has become a favorite form of robbery: follow the victim home, hit quick, go.

They came after Kathleen Kent in a red car, followed her as she drove from the bank to her home, which is on Ludlam Road, a block from South Miami Senior High.

Mrs. Kent described to me what happened:

School was letting out for the afternoon. Traffic was heavy, the area alive with students, two school buses, parents in cars waiting to pick up their kids.

She turned into her driveway, opened the automatic garage doors, drove in. The red car pulled into the driveway next door and a man got out. As Kathleen stepped from her own car in the garage…

"Suddenly, he was attacking me. He grabbed my purse and pulled. It had a strap over my shoulder, and the strap wouldn't break. He hit me. I was screaming. I fell and lost consciousness for a few seconds.

"When I came to, he was dragging me out to the driveway, arms around me, swinging me."

She had fleeting impressions of people around, watching. People in cars. Students passing by. Spectators, open-mouthed. "Help me, please help me!" Nobody came. Nobody helped.

Then the attacker was gone, and the red car sped away. She yelled, "Somebody get his license number!" And she blacked out again.

Kathleen Kent had suffered a mild concussion. She also has a heart condition. "I woke up lying in my driveway. Everybody was gone. I was by myself. My shoes were off. My purse was gone, with $150 in it. An elderly man stopped in a van and stared at me. I said, 'Would you please help me?' He rolled up his window and drove away."

She stumbled to the house of a neighbor, who called the police.

Sgt. Kent, a 28-year police veteran now assigned to the courts detail, arrived home as officers were writing the report. "She had bruises and minor cuts, her legs and arms were skinned. She had a concussion. She was terrified."

That night, Kathleen Kent suffered a heart attack.

She spent three days in intensive care at South Miami Hospital.

Three months have gone by since the Jan. 5 incident. She has gained some physical strength, but there are deep wounds to the mind and spirit She is haunted by the fact that nobody—nobody—came to her aid.

She tried to call the principal of South Miami High, Dr. Warren G. Burchell, and talked to his secretary. Then she wrote him a letter.

Principal Burchell: "Mrs. Kent was upset because nobody helped her. I'm concerned about that too. I tried to call her back several times, without success. I sent a police officer from the school to talk with her. Whether he saw her or not, I don't know. This is not officially a school matter, but we are concerned."

Kathleen Kent says nobody from the school contacted her.

"She is devastated, very paranoid," said Sgt. Kent. "She won't leave the house, won't drive, doesn't want to go anywhere."

They found her empty wallet in a Liberty City garbage can, along with some discarded syringes and other drug paraphernalia.

"People had no compassion," said Kent. "She had to crawl to her neighbor's for help. I wouldn't expect anyone to go after a strong-arm robber barehanded, but at least show some interest."

Paraphrase a verse from Leviticus 19 that applies to the article above.

SESSIONS FIVE AND SIX

In my class, *Jewish Life After Confirmation*, we explore the topic of interfaith dating and marriage. This is a very delicate subject as many of our students are products of interfaith marriages or marriages in which one parent is a Jew by choice, or have a parent who is in a second marriage with a non-Jew. This is a high-risk lesson—one which I would not advise for everyone. It is very important that all of the participants feel comfortable. No one should feel threatened, unwanted or rejected.

OBJECTIVES:

1. The parents and students will view a video on interfaith marriage and will react to it through guided discussion.

2. The students will interview their parents to determine parental views on interfaith dating and marriage. The students will react to their parents' responses.

PROCEDURE;

1. The teacher introduces herself to the parents. The students introduce their parents to the teacher and class.

2. The teacher gives a brief overview of course objectives and introduces the topic for the evening—interfaith dating and marriage. This introduction should include statistics on interfaith marriage and conversions, U.A.H.C. Outreach, problems that arise, the Basic Judaism course given at the temple for those interested in conversion, etc. Parents and students are drawn into a brief discussion of the problems that arise. The teacher states the reasons for including this topic in the course.

3. The video, *Intermarriage, This Great Difference*, from the U.A.H.C. (13 minute version), is introduced. The class is guided to observe the following:
    a. Background of the main characters
    b. What we know about each character
    c. How they change form the beginning of the video to the end
    d. Feelings expressed by each character
    f. Class reaction to video

4. The video is viewed.

5. The video is discussed, using the video guide and the list in #3 above

6. Students are given an interview worksheet, pair with their parent or parents, and complete the form. Students without a parent in class are "adopted" by others so that they can listen to an interview. These students will do the interview at home and return it the following week.

7. Parents and students regroup as a class and react to the exercise using the following questions as guidelines.

STUDENTS:
What did you learn about your parents' views that surprised you? How did you feel about it? Where did you agree or disagree?

PARENTS:
How did you feel sharing your views with your child? What surprised you in your dialogue? Was this a valuable exercise? What did you learn about yourself?

NOTE: *The purpose of this exercise is to foster communication in the family about interfaith marriage—its effect on those involved and on the Jewish community. It is a vehicle that can promote understanding of the problems involved and responses to them. Interfaith marriage is a reality. I believe that the time to discuss it is now when our students are beginning to date. Now is the time to discover family feelings, rather than later when one becomes more involved or engaged.*

Parent and student reactions have been powerful and interesting. Some of the students had heard their parents' views before the lesson and were not surprised at their responses. Others have been shocked at their parents' depth of feeling about the subject. Sometimes the participants really disagree with each other's views. Some parents are uncomfortable with the questions because they are caught (like Tevye) between belief and wanting their child to be happy. Most have a problem with "How would you feel if I converted to the other person's religion? Would you come to my wedding if I chose to marry in a church?" Parents are happy that they have the opportunity to discuss the topic with their child. Those who are Jews by choice or who are non-Jews have shared personal experiences of the problems that they faced and how they resolved or did not resolve them. Others shared about family members who were involved.

INTERVIEW OUTLINE

To the Student:

Please interview both parents, if this is possible. Interview them separately. Fill out the interview sheet. Bring all involved together to discuss the contents and to share feelings.

1. How do you feel about my dating a person who is not Jewish? _____
    _____

2. What are the reasons for your answer? _____
    _____

3. How would you feel if I married a person who was not Jewish ? _____
    If the person converted? _____
    If the person did not convert? _____
    If I converted to the other person's religion? _____

4. What would you as the parent do? _____
    _____

5. Can you give me reasons why you feel I should not marry someone who is not Jewish?
    _____

6. For a daughter: Would you give me a wedding if I chose to marry in a church? Why?____
    _____
    Why not? _____

7. For a son or daughter: Would you come to my wedding if I chose to marry in a church?
    Why? _____
    Why not? _____

INVOLVING STUDENTS

You have probably noticed in all of the activities that have been discussed that there is a high level of student involvement. The teacher creates the lesson, sets the parameters with specific directions and expectations and then involves each student. Remember, students want to be involved. They do not want to be lectured. They want to be a part of the learning process. They want to use more than their ears and eyes. They want to "do."

I totally enjoy the following activity. It did not happen all at once. It evolved after trying to achieve the results in many other ways.

WHAT DO WE KNOW INVENTORY:

This inventory is used after our session on interfaith dating and marriage and after we discuss the results of the parent interviews. One of the things we discuss is why our parents want us to marry Jews.

The class is told that since the beginning session of our course, we have been trying to get to know each other better. We have learned each other's names, what schools we attend, what we like to do, what we believe and what our parents believe. But even before we did all this there were certain things that we already knew about each other...sight unseen. "In fact", I say, "I know so much about you that it would boggle your mind. You know so much about each other that you would be surprised." (By this time, the teacher has everyone's full attention.)

I continue with, "Let me ask you a few questions. Raise your hand if you agree. Then look around. Are you surprised at your classmates' answers?"

I then read each item on the inventory and give the students the opportunity to respond. Each statement is usually discussed.

QUESTION 1. Usually everyone has a mezuzah on at least one doorpost. The attitude is, "Of course, we all have one." But, we have had students that did not. Recently a student from each of two classes did not. Both were from mixed marriages and had chosen to become Jews and attend our school in junior high. They shared why they made this choice and how Confirmation is different for them... more special because they chose to be confirmed as opposed to fulfilling a parent's wish.

The students' reactions are interesting. Questions 4,5,6,13, and 16 usually do not bring immediate response from everyone. Then the remembering begins. "Oh yes, I remember. When we were in Religious School we did that." "You do that when you are little."

"We always had punch and cookies in the sukkah." "I remember when my dad carried the big

WHAT DO WE KNOW INVENTORY

How many of you:

1. have a mezuzah on at least one door of your home?   _____
2. attend at least one religious service for the High Holidays?_____
3. fast on Yom Kippur?_____
4. have brought fruit to hang in a sukkah?_____
5. have eaten a snack or meal in a sukkah?_____
6. would know what to do with a *lulav* and *etrog*?_____
7. have marched in a Simhat Torah parade around the temple?_____
8. light the candles during Hanukkah?_____
9. have received presents on Hanukkah?_____
10. know the story of Hanukkah and can tell it?_____
11. can say or sing the Hanukkah blessings?_____
12. can sing "Rock of Ages," "I Have A Little Dreidel," or "Oh Hanukkah"?_____
13. have planted a tree in Israel on *Tu Bish'vat,* or have planted a tree with your hands while in Israel?
14. have visited or plan to visit Israel?_____
15. really care if Israel survives?_____
16. have dressed in a costume on Purim?_____
17. have eaten *hamantashen* on Purim?_____
18. know and can tell the story of Queen Esther?_____
19. attend at least one Seder during Passover?_____
20. do not eat bread or other forbidden foods on Passover?_____
21. know and can tell the Passover story?_____
22. can recite the Four Questions?_____
23. can list all ten of the Ten Commandments?_____
24. can participate in the Shabbat evening and morning service?_____
25. can chant the blessings before and after the reading of the Torah?_____
26. have contributed to a *tzedakah* project?_____
27. have parents who belong to a Jewish organization?_____
28. know your Hebrew names?_____(Call on each to recite it)
29. have Shabbat in your home _____every week?_____occasionally?_____never?
30. can recite the blessing over candles, wine, hallah for Shabbat?_____
31. have parents who light candles for someone who has died?_____
32. can recite kaddish?_____
33. identify with the Jewish people, its problems and joys?_____
34. really are concerned with the survival of Judaism?_____

Torah and I carried a little one." "I was always Queen Esther on Purim."

Questions 6, 10, 11, 12, 18, 21, 22, 25, 30, 32 are the most fun. Here the students begin to shake their pretend *lulav*, recite the blessings, tell stories, sing songs and do whatever action is described. They help each other with the words and correct each other when necessary. They really get into remembering.

Question 23 has the whole class working together to name the commandments. Usually they remember nine and someone always runs to the Bible to find the elusive commandment.

By this time the class is totally involved.

Were they surprised by what they knew? Are they surprised that the others in the class have had the same experiences? How do they feel about these experiences? Do they want to continue them and pass them on to their children? Would their parents want them to pass them on? Perhaps they can now see one of the reasons why parents get so uptight when teens begin to date out of the religion. There is so much that we have in common before we even exchange names. We are a part of a people. Our parents want to share these things with the grandchildren.

NOTE: Other questions that can be discussed include the following:

1. What is the purpose of rituals and traditions? How do they enhance our lives? What effect do they have on family? What is their impact on the survival of the Jewish people?

2. How would you feel if we did not have rituals and traditions?

3. Do we need rituals and traditions to connect with our Judaism?

4. Do you feel a connection with others in this room because you have had so many of the same experiences?

5. If someone in this class came to your home on Passover or Hanukkah, would you need to explain the rituals to them?

What about the child who cannot answer yes to anything listed? These students come to realize that they can make the decision to do and partake of everything. As they mature they will make these decisions for themselves. I share with the class that I grew up in a house where we rarely observed Shabbat, but as a young adult I chose to make Shabbat a part of my lifestyle and was attracted to my husband in part because ritual was a very definite part of his lifestyle.

THE FINAL TEST

The following is the final test that has been used with the course *Jewish Life After Confirmation*. The students take the workbook home the week before the test is given. Students who are absent are sent the workbook by mail.

This test was designed to discover the concepts and attitudes that the student now holds. The test provides the teacher with the opportunity to ascertain whether her objectives for the course were accomplished. The test gives the student the opportunity to recall and organize those concepts that were covered in class. This test is a communication device—the student shares herself and the teacher, during evaluation, shares herself.

The questions are organized to "jar" the students' memories as to where we have been and to help them remember what was covered. The questions are listed by weeks and with a statement that reminds the student what we did during that session. These statements remind the student of the different activities that they experienced. They reinforce that it was not "the same old thing" each week.

The students are seated in a scattered structure throughout the room instead of the usual semicircle. They are told that the teacher wants them to do well on the test. She will do everything she can to help with questions and concerns about the test. When a student has a question, she can bring her paper to the desk (an extra chair is provided), and the teacher will discuss it with her. There will be no talking to classmates during the test. Parents will be sent the evaluated test.

The students are told that it will take about a week to evaluate the tests as no more than five or six are evaluated at one sitting. Students will not be compared to others, only to themselves and what the teacher thinks she can expect from each one. There will be no grades, no numbers, no percentages. Each question will be evaluated on its own. If a student does not answer a section or a significant question correctly, the student will receive information and then will have to retake that part of the test. NO ONE WILL FAIL. The students are told to write as much as they can on a subject. The teacher will react and write also.

The teacher reviews each section of the test with the students. Week 1 is opinion. There are no right or wrong answers. The teacher wants to know what the student gained from this activity and its continuation throughout the weeks.

THE FINAL TEST

WEEK ONE:

We began our course with an exercise in awareness. You were given a leaf of your very own to study, to enjoy, to make yours. At the end of the exercise the leaf was taken away and destroyed.

    A.   What did you become aware of during this exercise?

    B.   How can this new awareness be applied to your life?

    C.   List three or four "leaves" that we discussed in class.

WEEKS TWO AND THREE:

We filled out a questionnaire. Some of the questions were about Confirmation. During the next few weeks we explored the concept of Confirmation and what it means to us. We tried to formulate a belief system.

    A.   Which branch of Judaism introduced the ceremony of Confirmation?

    B.   Why do Reform Jews put more emphasis on Confirmation than bar mitzvah?

    C.   What is the purpose of Confirmation?

    D.   Confirmation takes place on the holiday of _____which observes the event of _____.

    E.   We explored the idea that Moses, when accepting the Ten Commandments, did so not only for his contemporary Hebrews, but for all the generations to come.
         What does this mean to you as you near your own Confirmation?

    F.   We discussed the basic ideas of Judaism. Write one paragraph that you could read (with honesty) to the congregation on Confirmation morning that would express your beliefs at this time of your life. (God, responsibility, actions versus faith, chosen people, values, survival of Judaism.) Be specific.

WEEK FOUR:

We participated in a reaction and decision making exercise. We read situation cards and reacted to them immediately. We read passages from the book of Leviticus which began, "Ye shall be Holy for I the Lord your God am Holy." The purpose of this exercise was to share some of the moral laws of Judaism with you so that you could use them for a guide in your life of decision making.

READ THE TWO FOLLOWING SITUATIONS:

There are two answers to each of the following situations. Be sure to do as instructed.

NOTE: *The students are told that "2F" is the most important question on the test. It will require thought and honesty.*

VENDOR SHOT CHILDREN TAKE HIS ICE CREAM

CHICAGO—(AP)—More than 100 youngsters came running when an ice cream vendor was shot twice in a $75 robbery. But instead of helping the wounded man, they helped themselves to his wares, leaving him bleeding for more than an hour until police arrived, he said.

"All of them came out holding the ice cream and surrounded me, but nobody seemed to get help", said Ebenezer Obomanu, who was listed in good condition Saturday at the University of Illinois Hospital.

"I yelled at them to stop, but it didn't do any good," he said Friday night in an interview from his hospital bed. "It took about 15 or 20 minutes for them to empty my truck. It was a great celebration."

"I lost about $195 worth of ice cream," said Obomanu, 25, a Nigerian native and graduate student who works summers driving the truck.

Capt. William Murphy, acting Monroe District police commander, said "a couple hundred people" were at the scene Thursday when he arrived.

"There were so many people standing around that we couldn't even see the truck from where we were," Murphy said. "There is no doubt the kids came and looted the ice cream truck."

"I never knew such a thing would happen," Obomanu said. The children, he said, were as young as two years old.

A 12-year-old boy in the neighborhood said: "I told my mama I would be right back, I was going to go and get some ice cream. I ran downstairs and pushed my way through and got some."

The boy said he did not know then that the driver was hurt. "When I found out, I felt like a thief," he said.

Obomanu's route for Alexander's Sunshine Ice Cream took him through some of Chicago's rougher neighborhoods.

While on the city's west side Thursday, Obomanu was accosted by two armed men who shot him. once in the shoulder and once in the back, took his money and left him bleeding near a housing project.

A. What would you have done if you were there? Why?

B. What Jewish law applies here?

It is 5:30. You go shopping at the grocery store for your mom. You are in a rush as you have to go to an important meeting at 6:30. You arrive home at 6:00 and unpack the groceries. You notice that in addition to your groceries you also have a $10.62 package of fresh shrimp, $3.25 chicken, $2.89 chopped meat, scallions, and mushrooms. They were packed in by mistake.

A. What would you have done if you were there? Why?

B. What Jewish law applies here?

WEEKS FIVE AND SIX:

We viewed the film *Intermarriage, This Great Difference,* interviewed our parents, and found out what we knew about each other.

A. Write one paragraph giving reasons for dating and marrying a Jewish partner. Make your reasons strong enough to convince a friend.

B. Do you agree or disagree with your reasons? Why?

We viewed a videotape of a wedding in our sanctuary.

What are three symbols used in a Jewish wedding? What is their significance?

A. _____   A. _____

B. _____   B _____

C. _____   C. _____

During the wedding ceremony, the rabbi speaks of a covenant. What does this symbolize and who is it between?

WEEK SEVEN AND EIGHT: (*These lessons are not described in this volume*)

The questions in this next section require very definite answers. I read an article, "My Friend Don" to you. We discussed the stages of grief and the rituals associated with death.

A. Describe the basic philosophy behind Jewish death rituals.

B. Describe the *shiv'ah* period and its purpose.

C. What is yahrzeit? What do family members do on this occasion?

D. Describe an unveiling.

E. What is kaddish?

When is it said?

Who is commanded to say it?

F. How do we become immortal?

G. We began our course with LEAVES. We ended with LEAVES. We read Leo Buscaglia's *The Fall of Freddy the Leaf.* What did you learn from this story?

NOTE: *The theme of leaves has been a powerful motivator in this class. Ending this course with Freddy the Leaf's story has had a tremendous impact on the students. Many have checked it out in the library or have bought it to share with their parents and friends. I am encouraged to find similar themes for other courses that we use. It helps the student connect and remember.*

The last section of the test is the EVALUATION. The students are told that the teacher will spend many hours evaluating the answers on the test. She will write an evaluation paragraph at the end of the test about the student. This will include comments on attitude, participation, assignments, discussion, and attendance. If the teacher is taking time to do all this, then she would also appreciate the students taking time to evaluate her efforts. Students are asked to please take the time to complete these questions, and to be honest.

NOTE: *This evaluation can be stapled to the rest of the test or it can be done without a name. I have done it both ways and it has not made a difference in the responses. I have found that if there are good lines of communication, the students will be honest. If they do not like something or if they were bored with something they will write it. If the proper atmosphere has been established, the negatives will be given to help the teacher. They will not be angry or hostile. They will feel free to be honest. I personally like the evaluation included with the test so that I can respond to their comments.*

EVALUATION:

A. What are the main concepts that you learned from this course that you did not know previously?

B. What did you like best about this course?

C. What did you like least about this course?

D. What suggestions for improvement can you offer?

E. Was the booklet a helpful tool for learning?

The joy of this method of test giving is manifold. The parents love receiving the test. They read it very carefully. They usually do not have the opportunity to see what their child has learned and what their child really thinks about the subjects presented. They tell me that they discuss the questions and answers over dinner and they try to answer the questions from their point of view. I write very detailed comments about each student. The parents appreciate the time I take and that I care about their child. I know good things about their child and I share it.

The students know exactly how they performed in this course. They know what they have mastered and what they need to do to improve. They have the opportunity to do their best and to redo sections where improvement is necessary. They rarely have the opportunity to do this in other school settings. I send them strong messages. THEY ARE IMPORTANT. THEIR THOUGHTS ARE IMPORTANT. BEING JEWISH IS SPECIAL.

STUDENT RESPONSES TO COURSE EVALUATION QUESTIONS

A.   What are the main concepts that you learned from this course that you didn't already know?
—Traditions & certain Jewish morals & values.
—I learned about death marriage, & the everyday laws that are presented in the Bible.
—Concepts about death, what Confirmation really stands for.
—Concepts about death. An understanding of reasons for not inter-dating. What Confirmation means.
—How Jews go about death. Some marriage laws.
—I learned about death & how to go about it. A little about weddings.
—I learned so much in this class, I can't even begin to express it!
—Death, weddings, laws, etc. Things I never thought about or cared to. Most everything.
—Some of the traditions of the wedding & many traditions about burial & death.
—Death practices, marriage, Confirmation (purpose).
—The marriage ceremony, moral laws.
—About the funeral & how the Bible still applies today.
—I learned the important concepts of death, the proper way to handle it & why I am being confirmed.
—More on death & the symbolism of the Jewish wedding.
—I learned more about Jewish views of life & death. I also learned more about why I am getting confirmed.

B. What did you like best about this course?
—The teacher. You seemed to really enjoy teaching & that really affected me.
—I liked the way the information was presented to us in a very straightforward manner.
—The open discussions.
—The units about death. Thanks, it has helped me to go through my grandfather's illness.
—It was not boring.
—I liked learning about the deaths and how to go about it. I also liked the leaf exercise.
—I liked the movies we saw. They were interesting.
—Nothing specific. Just the whole experience.
—The part on death and the leaf exercise.
—We learned neat stuff, and you're an interesting teacher. Your materials (decision cards, leaves) were innovative & useful.
—The section on moral laws.
—The in-depth look at what we believe, especially about marriage and death.
—The leaf exercise. I enjoyed becoming aware of so many things by way of a simple, everyday leaf.
—That it was interesting.
—Discussing intermarriage & death.
—Learning about Jewish weddings & seeing films about intermarriage.
—Death

154

C. What did you like least about this course?

—Working from the Bible, but you used the everyday incidents to make it bearable.

—I thought that we should have moved a little bit quicker to get to finish more topics. We never got to finish whole topics.

—Nothing. The day when I disliked copying the verses from the Bible was the least pleasing.

—We had to write a lot.

—The things I didn't understand.

—I enjoyed it all.

—Again, nothing specific.

—When we did that part on the Bible.

—Leaving it.

D. What suggestions for improvement can you offer?

—Seriously, this course is one of the best thought-out, well-planned activities in the Temple.

—Quicker.

—Thanks, you've been wonderful. I can't remember enjoying a Religious School class this much.

—None. It was very good.

—I honestly don't know nor could help you.

—It's great.

—Unfortunately, I can not fairly judge the course because I never completed the entire book, or the course. As much as I would like to answer this question, I can't.

—Skip death (yuck)

—Spend more time on each subject.

—I don't think it needs improvements. It covered about everything dealing with life after Confirmation.

—A little more time to discuss things thoroughly.

—I think the class is good as it is now.

E. Was the booklet a helpful tool for learning?

—Yes, to a degree. But I think if there was more discussion, it would have been better.

—Definitely. Helped to visualize what we were learning.

—Yes. It was a good study guide & a good keepsake.

—Yes! It was a wonderful way to help pull the course together.

—Yes. I read through it at home & so did my Mom. She was very impressed.

—Definitely. The booklet was an efficient study aid. Continue to use it. I would value the booklet even more if we had finished it.

—Yes. The questions brought out what I knew but couldn't put in words.

—The course was more important, without the course the book wouldn't have helped.

—Yes. Whenever I had a question or just wanted to know something, it was always there. It was like a small journal of the course. It made studying rather simple.

—Yes. It helped in studying & gave me spaces to take notes on.

CHARTING STUDENTS' EVALUATION OF COURSE

CONCLUSIONS FROM TENTH GRADE EVALUATIONS:

1. What are the main concepts that you learned from this course that you did not already know?

    Students mentioned all of the areas of the course that were covered…Confirmation, interfaith marriage, death, beliefs, rituals, Jewish diseases etc. The unit on death appeared to have made the greatest impact. This was probably due to high interest and a lack of previous knowledge.

2. What did you like best about the course?

    The students mentioned the different methodology that was used to teach the basic concepts. They responded to open discussions and being able to share their own feelings. The subject of death was mentioned again which points up the need for death rituals and philosophy to be included in the school curriculum.

3. What did you like least about this course?

    The major area listed had to do with writing. The course comes at night after a long day at school. Discussions are more appealing than book work. Overall, the feelings were not negative.

4. What suggestions for improvement can you offer?

    The major offering is about time and depth of subject matter. Each subject area should be reviewed. Should sections of the curriculum be eliminated? Should the course be structured for more detail and fewer subject areas? The methodology used and approved by the students gives them the opportunity for maximum participation. Less participation would not solve the problem. More text and tighter control would not be welcomed. A balance must be achieved. Try experimenting with each lesson.

5. Was the booklet a helpful tool for learning?

    The students were very positive about using the booklet. They did not view it as "more school writing." It helped them to review and to organize. I liked the idea of sharing it with parents. Review the course and delete those pages that will not be used. Extra pages give the student the message that the teacher could not cover all of the material.

21.
THE ART OF EFFECTIVE TEACHING

The key to effective teaching is the planning process that takes place before we even step into our classrooms. The more we know about our school, the children and our own expectations, the more we will succeed. The days of "barber shop reading," where each child reads a paragraph when it is her turn, are over. The teacher cannot walk into class and "wing it." A teacher can no longer stay one chapter ahead of the students and hope to succeed. She cannot emulate her high school teachers and college professors and lecture to her students.

Today's Religious School students need to be "turned on" to Judaism. Religious School teachers are usually the prime source of their Jewish learning and experience. We must make an impact. The future of Judaism for the next generation depends upon us. This is an awesome responsibility.

Religious School teachers must plan, plan, plan. We must realize that we cannot do it all. We will be frustrated because of the lack of time, our own lack of knowledge, and a decline in commitment to Jewish education on the part of community. In spite of all of this, we have available to us excellent experiential methodology and strategies. We have the power to create a memorable learning experience for our students. They will not remember everything that we teach, but if we can create an environment of warmth, friendship, learning, scholarship, and enjoyment we will be able to reach many of our goals and objectives. This is our challenge.

One of the major goals of Religious Schools is to provide knowledge and positive Jewish experiences so that our students will marry Jewish people and become a part of the Jewish community—join a temple, send their child to Religious School, join Jewish organizations, support Israel, etc. Most teachers do not have the opportunity to see these goals realized.

I have been at Temple Beth Am for many years. My ex-students are now joining the temple and giving us their children to educate. Recently, the second generation of b'nai mitzvah students were called to the Torah. The president of our congregation was confirmed at our temple. Many of our graduates are leaders in the Jewish community—on the Board of Directors at Federations, the Jewish Community Center and other Jewish organizations. The teaching staff has had the pleasure of welcoming their own students to our faculty. These are young people who trained and worked in our school as teaching assistants, attended universities, and have come back to us to share their knowledge and commitment to the survival of Judaism with the next generation. These young people, who are evidence of our reaching our goals, are our future. We as teachers must continue to plan for our success and for theirs.

BIBLIOGRAPHY

READINGS THAT ARE HELPFUL

Alper, Janice P. ed. LEARNING TOGETHER: A SOURCEBOOK ON JEWISH FAMILY EDUCATION. Denver: Alternatives in Religious Education, 1987.

Bloom, Benjamin S., ed. TAXONOMY OF EDUCATIONAL OBJECTIVES. Handbook I: Cognitive Domain. New York: David Mckay Col, Inc., 1956.

Brimm, Jack, et al. "Principal's Attitudes: Student Absenteeism; A Survey Report. NAASP BULLETIN. 1978. 62, 65—9.

Dean, V.S. "Simulation: A Tool for In-Service Education." EDUCATIONAL LEADERSHIP. April 1981, 550-552.

DeBrun, Robert L. and Jack L. Larson. YOU CAN HANDLE THEM ALL. Kansas: Master Teacher Inc., 1984

Elkins, Dov P. CLARIFYING JEWISH VALUES. Rochester, New York: Growth Associates, 1977.

Gagne, Robert M. LEARNING AND INDIVIDUAL DIFFERENCES. Columbus, Ohio: Charles E. Merrill, 1966.

Glasser, William. SCHOOLS WITHOUT FAILURE. New York: Harper and Row, 1969.

Gordon, Dr. Thomas, T.E.T.: TEACHER EFFECTIVENESS TRAINING. New York: Peter H. Wyden, 1974.

Griggs, Donald L. TEACHING TEACHERS TO TEACH. California: Griggs Educational Service, 1974.

Herman, Dorothy C. EXPERIENTIAL METHODOLOGY IN TEACHER TRAINING. Miami: Central Agency for Jewish Education, 1977.

.......FROM GENERATION TO GENERATION. Miami: CAJE, 1985

.......THE JOY OF SHABBAT. Miami: CAJE, 1982.

.......TOURING ISRAEL. Miami: CAJE, 1979.

Krathwohl, David R. Benjamin S. Bloom, and Bertram B. Masia TAXONOMY OF EDUCATIONAL OBJECTIVES, Handbook II: Effective Domain. New York: David Mcakay Co., 1964.

Madsen, Charles H. Jr. and Clifford K. Madsen. TEACHING DISCIPLINE. Boston: Allyn and
  Bacon, 1970.

Mager, Robert F. PREPARING INSTRUCTIONAL OBJECTIVES. California: Fearson Publishers,
  1962.

Marcus, Audrey F. JEWISH TEACHERS HANDBOOK VOL. 1,2,3. Denver: Alternatives in Jewish
  Education. 1980, 1981, 1982.

Marcus, Audrey F. and Raymond A. Zwerin, ed. THE JEWISH PRINCIPAL'S HANDBOOK.
  Denver: 1983.

MASTER TEACHER. Leadership Lane, P.O. BOX 1207, Manhattan, Kansas 66502.

Taba, Hilda. CURRICULUM DEVELOPMENT: THEORY AND PRACTICE. New York: Harcourt
  Brace Jovanavich, Inc., 1962.

Tyler, Ralph W. BASIC PRINCIPLES OF CURRICULUM AND INSTRUCTION. Chicago: The
  University of Chicago Press, 1949.

Weinstein, C.S. "Physical Environment of the School: "Review of Research." REVIEW OF EDU-
  CATIONAL RESEARCH. fall 1979, 49, 571-610.

Wolfgang, Charles H. and Carl D. Glickman. SOLVING DISCIPLINE PROBLEMS. Boston: Allyn
  and Bacon, 1980.